This book belongs to:

Name

School

Full Name	Age & Birthday

ABOUT ME

Today I am....

☐ Happy   ☐ Bubbly   ☐ Tickled   ☐ Joyous

QUESTIONS	ANSWERS
Hair Color	
Eye Color	
Height	
Where were you born?	
Do you have any pets?	
What is your favorite food(s)?	
Do you have any brothers and sisters?	

What do you want to be when you grow up?

What is your favorite subject in school?

What do you like to do in your free time?

What makes you unique?

4th Grade Grammar Overview:
Nouns, Verbs, Adjectives

A noun is a word that describes someone, a place, something, or an idea. Names, locations, physical objects, or objects and concepts that do not exist in the physical world, such as a dream or a theory, are examples of nouns. A noun is a single word, such as sister, home, desk, wedding, hope, pizza, or squirrel.

There are numerous ways to use nouns in language, and these various types of nouns are classified. In general, there are ten distinct types of nouns that are used in specific and unique contexts, but let's look at eight of them today.

Common Noun	a non-specific person, place, or thing	baby, mom
Compound Nouns	made up of two nouns	bus driver, sunflower
Collective Noun	group of individuals	team, family
Proper Noun	A specific person, place, or thing	Dr. Morgan, Amazon
Concrete Noun	identified through one of the five senses	air, chirps
Plural Noun	Multiple people, places, or things	bottles, pencils
Singular Noun	One person, place, or thing	chair, desk
Abstract Noun	things that don't exist as physical objects	fear, love

Common Noun: A generic name for a person, place, or thing in a class or group is a common noun. In contrast to proper nouns, common nouns are not capitalized unless they begin a sentence or appear in a title. All nouns fall into one of two categories: common or proper. Proper nouns are distinct from common nouns in that they name something specific. Nouns in common use do not. Unnecessary capitalization of common nouns is a common spelling error. Some words, such as president, seem to beg for a capital letter because we instinctively want to emphasize their significance. However, if it does not name something or someone specific, even this lofty title is a common noun (in this case, a specific president).

Compound Noun: Every compound noun is made up of two or more words that are combined to form a noun. These distinct words do not have to be nouns in and of themselves; all they need to do is communicate a specific person, place, idea, or thing. A compound noun can be a common noun (for example, fish sticks), a proper noun (for example, Pizza Hut), or an abstract noun (lovesickness). They can be hyphenated or not, and they can have a space between words—especially if one of the words has more than one syllable, as in living room. You'll start noticing compound nouns everywhere once you've learned to recognize them. Fire-flies? Compound noun. Sub sandwich? Compound noun. Software developer, mother-in-law, underworld, toothache, garlic knot? They are all compound nouns.

Collective Noun: A collective noun is a word or phrase that refers to a group of people or things as if they were a single entity. There are some exceptions to the rule that collective nouns are treated as singular. Collective nouns such as team, family, class, group, and host use a singular verb when the entity acts as a whole and a plural verb when the individuals who make up the entity act individually.

Collective nouns refer to more than one person or thing in a category. A pride cannot have just one lion, and a single flower does not make a bouquet. As a result, a collective noun always refers to a plurality of some kind.

Example: The group is working on a mural. (Because the mural is painted collectively by the group, the verb is singular.)

Example: The group cannot agree on how to paint the mural. (Because the group members disagree with one another, the verb is plural.)

Proper Noun: A proper noun is a name that is specific (as opposed to generic) to a specific person, place, or thing. In English, proper nouns are always capitalized, regardless of where they appear in a sentence. That is, whether it appears at the beginning, middle, or end of a sentence, it is always written with the first letter in capital letters. In a sentence, a proper noun is used to name a person, place, or organization, such as Jim, Molly, India, Germany, Amazon, Microsoft, and so on.

Concrete Noun: A concrete noun is one that can be identified using at least one of the five senses (taste, touch, sight, hearing, or smell). Objects and substances that we cannot perceive (see, hear, taste, touch, or smell) with our sense organs are NOT concrete nouns. The majority of nouns become concrete nouns because we can feel them (for example, all animals and people) with our sense organs. Concrete nouns can be common nouns, countable nouns, proper nouns, uncountable nouns, collective nouns, and so on. All nouns are classified into two types: concrete nouns and abstract nouns.

Abstract Nouns: An abstract noun is one that cannot be perceived through any of the five senses (i.e., taste, touch, sight, hearing, smelling). In other words, an abstract noun is a noun that exists only in our minds and cannot be recognized by our senses.

Concrete nouns are tangible, whereas abstract nouns are intangible.

Concrete nouns can be experienced with the five senses, whereas abstract nouns cannot.

Singular Noun: Singular nouns are used in sentences to refer to a single person, place, thing, or idea. Singular nouns include things like boy, girl, teacher, boat, goat, hand, and so on.

Plural noun: There are numerous plural noun rules, and because nouns are used so frequently in writing! The correct spelling of plurals is usually determined by what letter the singular noun ends in. Take a look at some examples.

Add s to the end of regular nouns to make them plural.

cat – cats

house – houses

If the singular noun ends in s, ss, sh, ch, x, or z, add es to make it plural.

bus – buses

lunch – lunches

Singular nouns ending in -s or -z may require you to double the -s or -z before adding the -es for pluralization in some cases.

quiz – quizzes

gas –gasses

If the noun ends in f or fe, the f is frequently changed to ve before adding the -s to form the plural form.

calf–calves

wife – wives

Exceptions:

roof – roofs

hef – chefs

When some nouns are pluralized, they do not change at all.

heep – sheep

pecies – species

There are additional rules that we did not cover here. Please spend some time studying the following:

the final letter of a singular noun is -y and the letter preceding the -y is a consonant, the noun ends in -y. puppy - puppies

the singular noun ends in -y and the letter preceding the -y is a vowel, add an -s. boy – boys

the singular noun ends in -o, make it plural by adding -es. potato – potatoes Exception: photo – photos

a singular noun ends in -us, the plural ending is usually -i. cactus – cacti

When a singular noun ends in -is, the plural ending is -es. ellipsis – ellipses

a singular noun ends in -on, the plural noun ends in -a. criterion – criteria

Verbs

In theory, verbs are easy to understand. A verb is a word that describes an action, an occurrence, or a state of being. Of course, there are many different types of verbs, but remember that a verb should indicate that something is happening because an action is taking place in some way. When first learning about verbs, many students simply refer to them as 'doing words,' because they always indicate that something has been done, is being done, or will be done in the future (depending on the tense that you are writing in).

Verbs, like nouns, are the main part of a sentence or phrase, telling a story about what is going on. In fact, full thoughts cannot be conveyed without a verb, and even the simplest sentences, such as (Kim sings.) Actually, a verb can be a sentence in and of itself, with the subject, in most cases you, implied, as in Sing! and Drive!

The location of the verb in relation to the subject is one clue that can help you identify it. Verbs are almost always followed by a noun or pronoun. The subject is made up of these nouns and pronouns.

1. Jim **eats** his dinner quickly.
2. We **went** to the bank.

Adjectives

Adjectives are descriptive words for nouns. A noun is defined as a person, place, thing, or idea. We want to be as descriptive as possible when we speak or write. Being descriptive allows the reader or listener to understand better what you are attempting to describe. You want your audience to have the best possible understanding of what you're describing.

What image comes to mind when I say, "I saw a cat?" You might see a spotted cat, a small orange cat, or a shaggy gray cat, depending on your experience. I didn't give you enough adjectives to paint a complete picture.

Do you have a better mental image if I say, "I saw a big, wet, sad, shaggy, orange and white cat"? Of course, you do because I used adjectives to clarify things.

4th Grade Grammar: Nouns, Verbs, Adjectives

DIRECTIONS: SORT the words (below) by their corresponding *part-of-speech*.

color	chickens	kittens	banjo	library	goldfish
grieving	adorable	cough	stand	nasty	powerful
dance	build	cry	break	easy	circle
coach	aggressive	careful	eat	adventurous	think
mysterious	face	sticks	drink	guitar	busy
calm	window	worm	coast	draw	polka dot
eager	handsome	explain			

Nouns (13)	Verbs (13)	Adjectives (13)

*Usage Activity: CHOOSE (12) words from your completed table & WRITE (1) sentence for each form of the words you chose.

4th Grade Grammar: Compound Nouns

A compound noun is one that is composed of two or more words. Each word contributes to the meaning of the noun.

Compound nouns can be written three ways:

A single word	Two words	Hyphenated
haircut	rain forest	self-esteem

Instructions: Match the compound noun pairs correctly.

#				
1	[ ]	Fund	crow	
2	[ ]	News	dresser	
3	[ ]	Sun	glasses	
4	[ ]	Child	paper	
5	[ ]	Door	attack	
6	[ ]	heart	hood	
7	[ ]	tooth	plane	
8	[ ]	apple	cut	
9	[ ]	full	ring	
10	[ ]	hair	paste	
11	[ ]	air	sauce	
12	[ ]	ear	book	
13	[ ]	scare	moon	
14	[ ]	post	way	
15	[ ]	hair	raiser	
16	[ ]	note	office	

4th Grade Grammar: Collective Noun

A collective noun is a noun that refers to a group of people, animals, or things. They are described as a single entity. Collective nouns are distinct from singular nouns in that singular nouns describe only one person or object.

Many collective nouns are common nouns, but when they are the name of a company or other organization with more than one person, such as Microsoft, they can also be proper nouns.

Find the collective noun in each sentence.

1. Our class visited the natural history museum on a field trip.

2. The bison herd stampeded across the prairie, leaving a massive dust cloud in its wake.

3. We eagerly awaited the verdict of the jury.

4. This year's basketball team features three players who stand taller than six feet.

5. At Waterloo, Napoleon's army was finally defeated.

6. The plans for a new park have been approved by the town council.

7. He comes from a large family, as the oldest of eleven children.

8. The rock group has been on tour for several months.

9. When Elvis appeared on stage, the entire audience erupted in applause.

10. The San Francisco crowd were their usual individualistic selves.

11. The crew of sailors boarded the ships.

12. A mob destroyed the company's new office.

13. The fleet of ships was waiting at the port.

14. It was difficult for the committee to come to a decision.

4th Grade Grammar: Concrete & Abstract Noun

In the English language, both concrete and abstract nouns are essential parts of speech. The primary distinction between concrete and abstract nouns is that concrete nouns refer to people, places, or things that take up physical space, whereas abstract nouns refer to intangible ideas that cannot be physically interacted with.

Words like "luck," "disgust," and "empathy" are examples of abstract nouns. While it is possible to see someone being empathetic, empathy is not a visible or tangible entity. The majority of feelings, emotions, and philosophies can be classified as abstract nouns.

1. FIND THE ABSTRACT NOUN
   a. KIND
   b. BOOK

2. FIND THE ABTRACT NOUN: THE KING WAS KNOWN FOR HIS JUSTICE
   a. JUSTICE
   b. KING

3. WHICH NOUN BELOW IS AN ABSTRACT NOUN?
   a. TRAIN
   b. LOVE

4. WHAT IS A CONCRETE NOUN?
   a. A NOUN THAT YOU CAN EXPERIENCE WITH AT LEAST 1 OF YOUR 5 SENSES.
   b. A NOUN THAT YOU CAN'T EXPERIENCE WITH AT LEAST 1 OF YOUR 5 SENSES.

5. WHICH WORD BELOW IS NOT A CONCRETE NOUN?
   a. HAMBURGER
   b. ANGER

2. FIND THE CONCRETE NOUNS
   a. WINDOW
   b. LOVE

4. WHAT ARE THE 5 CONCRETE NOUNS
   a. TASTE, SMELL, WALKING, EYEING, TOUCHING
   b. SMELL,TASTE, SIGHT, HEARING,TOUCH

6. IS THE FOLLOWING NOUN CONCRETE OR ABSTRACT? CUPCAKES
   a. ABSTRACT
   b. CONCRETE

8. WHICH WORD BELOW IS AN ABSTRACT NOUN?
   a. BRAVERY
   b. FRIEND

10. IS THE WORD THOUGHTFULNESS A CONCRETE OR ABSTRACT NOUN?
   a. ABSTRACT
   b. CONCRETE

Reading Bar Graphs

nswer the following questions based off the bar graph.

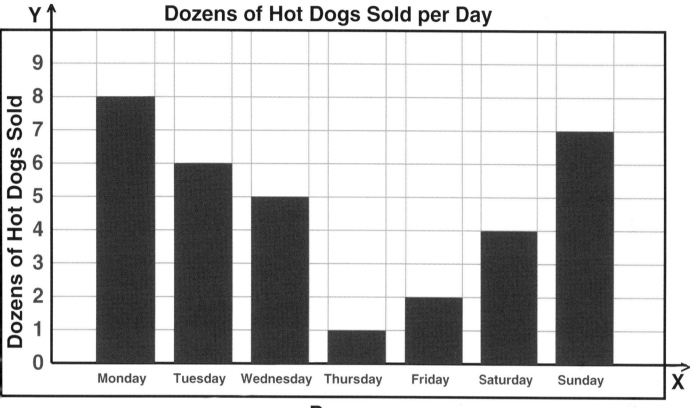

How many hot dogs were sold on Saturday and Tuesday combined?   _____

How many more hot dogs were sold on Monday than on Thursday?   _____

How many hot dogs were sold on Thursday, Friday, and Sunday?   _____

Next week, we hope to sell twice as many hot dogs as we did this week. How many hot dogs will that be?   _____

Were more hot dogs sold on Monday or on Thursday?   _____

Rounding rules:

Look at the digit to the right to round a number to the nearest ten place. If the number is five or more, round up. If the number is four or less, round down.

Round up if a number ends in 5, 6, 7, 8, or 9.
Round down if a number ends in 1, 2, 3, or 4.

For instance, 671 rounded to the nearest ten is 670 because the digit to the right of the tens place ended with one, so we round down.

Score : _____

Date : _____

Round each number to the nearest tens.

1) 712 $\longrightarrow$ 710
    - 397 $\longrightarrow$ - 400

    310

8) 484 $\longrightarrow$
    + 235 $\longrightarrow$ + _____

2) 428 $\longrightarrow$
    - 232 $\longrightarrow$ - _____

9) 939 $\longrightarrow$
    + 548 $\longrightarrow$ + _____

3) 716 $\longrightarrow$
    + 479 $\longrightarrow$ + _____

10) 692 $\longrightarrow$
     + 542 $\longrightarrow$ + _____

4) 514 $\longrightarrow$
    + 133 $\longrightarrow$ + _____

11) 414 $\longrightarrow$
     + 921 $\longrightarrow$ + _____

5) 935 $\longrightarrow$
    - 188 $\longrightarrow$ - _____

12) 224 $\longrightarrow$
     - 154 $\longrightarrow$ - _____

6) 481 $\longrightarrow$
    + 131 $\longrightarrow$ + _____

13) 321 $\longrightarrow$
     - 257 $\longrightarrow$ - _____

7) 798 $\longrightarrow$
    - 647 $\longrightarrow$ - _____

14) 295 $\longrightarrow$
     - 182 $\longrightarrow$ - _____

Time

Score : _____

Date : _____

What time is on the clock?   _____

What time will it be in 4 hours and 20 minutes?   _____

What time was it 1 hour and 40 minutes ago?   _____

What time will it be in 3 hours ?   _____

What time is on the clock?   _____

What time will it be in 1 hour and 40 minutes?   _____

What time was it 2 hours and 20 minutes ago?   _____

What time will it be in 1 hour ?   _____

What time is on the clock?   _____

What time will it be in 3 hours and 40 minutes?   _____

What time was it 1 hour and 20 minutes ago?   _____

What time will it be in 4 hours ?   _____

What time is on the clock?   _____

What time will it be in 4 hours ?   _____

What time was it 2 hours and 20 minutes ago?   _____

What time will it be in 2 hours ?   _____

Write the Numbers in Standard Form.

1) __884__ 800 + 80 + 4

2) _____ 400 + 40 + 8

3) _____ 500 + 30 + 0

4) _____ 900 + 70 + 7

5) _____ 300 + 10 + 2

6) _____ 600 + 10 + 8

7) _____ 800 + 60 + 8

8) _____ 800 + 90 + 0

9) _____ 500 + 50 + 6

10) _____ 300 + 70 + 7

11) _____ 500 + 60 + 7

12) _____ 900 + 40 + 8

13) _____ 700 + 80 + 7

14) _____ 700 + 10 + 0

15) _____ 900 + 80 + 4

When we write the number 521, we are actually saying that we have a total of 500 + 20 + 1. The number has been expanded to show the value of each of its digits. We write a number in expanded form when we expand it to show the value of each digit.

When you calculate how long something takes, you are calculating the elapsed time. The difference between two times is referred to as elapsed time.

Elapsed time is calculated as elapsed time = end time – start time. Separately subtract the minutes and hours. Subtract 12:10 from 16:4 to calculate the elapsed time between 12:10 and 16:40. When you look at the hours, 16-12=4 and when you look at the minutes, 40-10=30. The time has passed in 4 hours and 30 minutes.

Score : _____

Date : _____

How Much Time Has Elapsed ?

1)   1:40 P.M.   to   7:35 P.M.   _____

2)   1:20 A.M.   to   6:49 A.M.   _____

3)   6:40 P.M.   to   8:24 P.M.   _____

4)   2:40 P.M.   to   12:31 A.M.   _____

5)   2:20 A.M.   to   5:46 A.M.   _____

6)   2:00 A.M.   to   10:14 A.M.   _____

7)   10:00 A.M.   to   12:57 P.M.   _____

8)   6:40 A.M.   to   10:17 A.M.   _____

9)   9:40 P.M.   to   1:52 A.M.   _____

0)   6:20 P.M.   to   11:57 P.M.   _____

1)   2:00 A.M.   to   3:45 A.M.   _____

2)   8:00 A.M.   to   2:54 P.M.   _____

3)   12:40 A.M.   to   2:50 A.M.   _____

4)   11:20 P.M.   to   8:39 A.M.   _____

5)   9:00 P.M.   to   1:58 A.M.   _____

Drawing Bar Graphs

Graph the given information as a bar graph below on the graph. You can use a pencil to shade in the graph.

Day	# of Hot Dogs Sold
Monday	96
Tuesday	24
Wednesday	48
Thursday	72
Friday	60
Saturday	36
Sunday	12

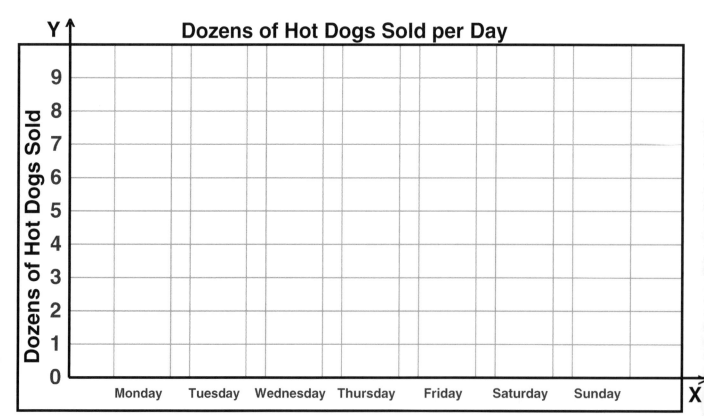

Dozens of Hot Dogs Sold per Day

Complete the Skip Counting Series

)   19,   17,   15,   13,   11,   9,   7,   5,   3,   1

)   74,   55,   36,   17,   -2,   -21,   -40,   -59,   -78,   -97

)   59,   50,   41,   32,   23,   14,   5,   -4,   -13,   -22

)   75,   80,   85,   90,   95,   100,   105,   110,   115,   120

)   88,   98,   108,   118,   128,   138,   148,   158,   168,   178

)   77,   86,   95,   104,   113,   122,   131,   140,   149,   158

)   86,   75,   64,   53,   42,   31,   20,   9,   -2,   -13

)   90,   75,   60,   45,   30,   15,   0,   -15,   -30,   -45

)   33,   28,   23,   18,   13,   8,   3,   -2,   -7,   -12

)   19,   27,   35,   43,   51,   59,   67,   75,   83,   91

)   20,   24,   28,   32,   36,   40,   44,   48,   52,   56

)   30,   27,   24,   21,   18,   15,   12,   9,   6,   3

Addition Worksheet

```
   53125          893724         7754653          40034
   58540          759775         8766279          70732
   79810          403688         7714657          43161
 + 11737        + 200969       + 4524724        + 41196
 _____        _____       _____        _____
```

```
  192189         2241377          84097          413796
  965026         7928905          19687          877734
  531938         5984195          69704          997766
 + 385320       + 8264879        + 21157        + 742703
 _____        _____        _____        _____
```

```
 7059169          86799          636053         6947438
 5369228          28259          120921         8770263
 9985601          90783          897238         9488267
 + 8707044       + 14295        + 447023       + 9910513
 _____        _____        _____        _____
```

```
   35283         189936         7019570          24476
   17919         753760         1010287          75122
   61158         617906         5621292          61687
 + 49632        + 863520       + 5479675        + 55646
 _____        _____       _____        _____
```

Find the Missing Number

Score : _____

Date : _____

33X23=759

1) N x 23 = 759   N = __33__

560/40=14

3) N ÷ 40 = 14   N = __560__

2) N - 23 = 16   N = ____

4) N - 14 = 1   N = ____

5) 34 + N = 55   N = ____

6) N - 17 = 13   N = ____

7) 25 - N = 4   N = ____

8) N x 22 = 770   N = ____

9) 17 + N = 49   N = ____

10) N - 37 = 3   N = ____

11) N ÷ 31 = 12   N = ____

12) 32 + N = 69   N = ____

13) 37 - N = 12   N = ____

14) 14 x N = 420   N = ____

15) N + 30 = 56   N = ____

16) N + 30 = 61   N = ____

17) 24 - N = 2   N = ____

18) 31 x N = 775   N = ____

19) 30 + N = 60   N = ____

20) N x 13 = 156   N = ____

21) N ÷ 21 = 38   N = ____

22) N ÷ 29 = 40   N = ____

23) 40 x N = 600   N = ____

24) N x 10 = 310   N = ____

25) 28 + N = 68   N = ____

26) 361 ÷ N = 19   N = ____

27) 253 ÷ N = 11   N = ____

28) 27 + N = 51   N = ____

29) N x 11 = 209   N = ____

30) N ÷ 32 = 36   N = ____

Division is the process of dividing a number into equal parts.

For instance, 20 divided by 4 =?
If you divide 20 items into four equal-sized groups, each
group will contain five items. The correct answer is 5.

Score : _____

Date : _____

$110 \div 10 =$

$35 \div 7 =$

$90 \div 9 =$

$3 \div 1 =$

$66 \div 11 =$

$9 \div 9 =$

$8 \div 4 =$

$60 \div 5 =$

$48 \div 8 =$

$45 \div 5 =$

$9 \div 3 =$

$90 \div 9 =$

$24 \div 12 =$

$24 \div 6 =$

$35 \div 5 =$

$48 \div 4 =$

$28 \div 4 =$

$12 \div 12 =$

$8 \div 1 =$

$60 \div 6 =$

$50 \div 10 =$

$4 \div 2 =$

$14 \div 2 =$

$132 \div 11 =$

$42 \div 7 =$

$22 \div 2 =$

$54 \div 6 =$

$80 \div 10 =$

$9 \div 3 =$

$40 \div 8 =$

A fraction is a portion of a whole. When something is divided into several parts, the fraction indicates how many of those parts you have.

The numerator is how many parts you have. The denominator is how many parts the whole was divided into.

Score : _____

Date : _____

What is the Fraction of the Shaded Area ?

1)   __3/4__

2)   _____

3)   _____

4)   _____

5)   _____

6)   _____

7)   _____

8)   _____

9)   _____

10)   _____

Shade the Figure with the Indicated Fraction.

11) $\dfrac{1}{2}$

12) $\dfrac{1}{4}$

13) $\dfrac{1}{5}$

14) $\dfrac{5}{8}$

15) $\dfrac{2}{8}$

16) $\dfrac{4}{8}$

17) $\dfrac{4}{5}$

18) $\dfrac{1}{8}$

19) $\dfrac{2}{4}$

20) $\dfrac{4}{5}$

4th Grade Science: Vertebrates

To begin, all animals are classified as either vertebrates or invertebrates. Invertebrates lack a backbone, whereas vertebrates do. Scientists can't stop there, because each group contains thousands of different animals! As a result, scientists divide vertebrates and invertebrates into increasingly smaller groups. Let's talk about vertebrates and some of their classifications.

Vertebrates range in size from a frog to a blue whale. Because there are at least 59,000 different types of vertebrates on the planet, they are further classified into five major groups: mammals, birds, fish, amphibians, and reptiles. Remember that animals are classified into these groups based on what they have in common. Why is an elephant classified as a mammal while a crocodile is classified as a reptile? Let's go over some of the characteristics of each vertebrate group.

Warm-blooded animals are mammals. This means that their bodies maintain their temperature, which is usually higher than the temperature of the surrounding air. They also have hair or fur; they have lungs to breathe air; that they feed milk to their babies; and that most give birth to live young rather than laying eggs, as a dog does.

- Birds have feathers, two wings (though not all birds, such as the ostrich and penguin, can fly), are warm-blooded, and lay eggs.
- Fish have fins or scales, live in water, and breathe oxygen through gills.
- Like salamanders and frogs, Amphibians have smooth, moist skin (amphibians must keep their skin wet); lay eggs in water; most breathe through their skin and lungs.
- Reptiles have scales (imagine a scaly lizard), are cold-blooded (their body temperature changes as the temperature around them changes), breathe air. Most reptiles, including the crocodile and snake, lay hard-shelled eggs on land.

Vertebrates play several vital roles in an ecosystem. Many predator species are large vertebrates in ecosystems. Lions, eagles, and sharks are examples of predatory vertebrates. Many prey species in ecosystems are also vertebrates. Mice, rabbits, and frogs are examples of these animals. Many vertebrates serve as scavengers in ecosystems. They are significant because they remove dead animals from the environment. Turkey vultures and hyenas, for example, are both vertebrate scavengers. Furthermore, many vertebrates serve as pollinators in ecosystems. Bats and monkeys, for example, may aid in pollen spread by visiting various trees and plants.

Humans value vertebrates for a variety of reasons. Vertebrates are domesticated animals used by humans. These animals are capable of producing milk, food, and clothing. They can also help with work. Agricultural animals are usually vertebrates. Humans also hunt a variety of wild vertebrate animals for food.

1. Vertebrates range in _____ from a frog to a blue whale.
   a. age
   b. size

2. Fish have fins or scales, live in water, and breathe ___ through gills.
   a. oxygen
   b. water

3. Invertebrates lack a _____, whereas vertebrates _____.
   a. skin, whereas vertebrates do
   b. backbone, whereas vertebrates do

4. Warm-blooded animals are _____.
   a. mammals
   b. producers

5. Some vertebrates serve as _____, they remove dead animals from the environment.
   a. scavengers
   b. invertebrates

6. Lions, eagles, and sharks are examples of _____ vertebrates.
   a. ecofriendly
   b. predatory

7. _____ animals are capable of producing milk, food, and clothing.
   a. Non-producing
   b. Domesticated

8. Many vertebrates serve as _____in ecosystems, they may aid in pollen spread by visiting various trees and plants.
   a. water lilies
   b. pollinators

4th Grade Science: Invertebrates

Invertebrates can be found almost anywhere. Invertebrates account for at least 95% of all animals on the planet! Do you know what one thing they all have in common? Invertebrates lack a backbone.

Your body is supported by a backbone, which protects your organs and connects your other bones. As a result, you are a vertebrate. On the other hand, invertebrates lack the support of bones, so their bodies are often simpler, softer, and smaller. They are also cold-blooded, which means their body temperature fluctuates in response to changes in the air or water around them.

Invertebrates can be found flying, swimming, crawling, or floating and provide essential services to the environment and humans. Nobody knows how many different types of invertebrates there are, but there are millions!

Just because an invertebrate lacks a spinal column does not mean it does not need to eat. Invertebrates, like all other forms of animal life, must obtain nutrients from their surroundings. Invertebrates have evolved two types of digestion to accomplish this. The use of intracellular digestion is common in the most simple organisms. The food is absorbed into the cell and broken down in the cytoplasm at this point. Extracellular digestion, in which cells break down food through the secretion of enzymes and other techniques, is used by more advanced invertebrates. All vertebrates use extracellular digestion.

Still, all animals, invertebrates or not, need a way to get rid of waste. Most invertebrates, especially the simplest ones, use the process of diffusion to eliminate waste. This is merely the opposite of intracellular digestion. However, more advanced invertebrates have more advanced waste disposal mechanisms. Similar to our kidneys, specialized glands in these animals filter and excrete waste. But there is a happy medium. Even though some invertebrates do not have complete digestive tracts like vertebrates, they do not simply flush out waste through diffusion. Instead, the mouth doubles as an exit.

Scientists have classified invertebrates into numerous groups based on what the animals have in common. Arthropods have segmented bodies, which means that they are divided into sections. Consider an ant!

Arthropods are the most numerous group of invertebrates. They can live on land, as spiders and insects do, or in water, as crayfish and crabs do. Because insects are the most numerous group of arthropods, many of them fly, including mosquitoes, bees, locusts, and ladybugs.

They also have jointed legs or limbs to help them walk, similar to how you have knees for your legs and elbows for your arms. The majority of arthropods have an exoskeleton, tough outer skin, or shell that protects their body. Have you ever wondered why when you squish a bug, it makes that crunching sound? That's right; it's the exoskeleton!

Mollusks are the second most numerous group of invertebrates. They have soft bodies and can be found on land or in water. Shells protect the soft bodies of many mollusks, including snails, oysters, clams, and scallops. However, not all, such as octopus, squid, and cuttlefish, have a shell.

1. Invertebrates lack a _____.
   a. backbone
   b. tailbone

2. Invertebrates are also _____.
   a. cold-blooded
   b. warm-blooded

3. _____ can live on land, as spiders and insects do, or in water, as crayfish and crabs do.
   a. Vertebrates
   b. Arthropods

4. All animals, invertebrates or not, need a way to get rid of _____.
   a. their skin
   b. waste

5. _____ have soft bodies and can be found on land or in water.
   a. Arthropods
   b. Mollusks

6. Just because an invertebrate lacks a _____ column does not mean it does not need to eat.
   a. spinal
   b. tissues

7. Your body is supported by a backbone, which protects your _____ and connects your other bones.
   a. organs
   b. muscles

8. Invertebrates lack the support of bones, so their bodies are often simpler, ___, and smaller.
   a. softer and bigger
   b. softer and smaller

4th Grade Science: Organelles

Do you and your dog have a similar appearance? We are all aware that people and dogs appear to be very different on the outside. However, there are some similarities on the inside. Cells make up all animals, including humans and dogs.

All animal cells appear to be the same. They have a cell membrane that contains cytoplasm, which is a gooey fluid. Organelles float in the cytoplasm. Organelles function as tiny machines that meet the needs of the cell. The term organelle refers to a "miniature organ." This lesson will teach you about the various organelles found in animal cells and what they do.

The nucleus of the cell is the cell's brain. It is in charge of many of the cell's functions. The nucleus is where DNA, the genetic instructions for building your body, is stored. DNA contains vital information! Your nucleus has its membrane to protect this essential information, similar to the membrane that surrounds the entire cell.

Your cells require energy. Energy is produced by mitochondria, which are oval-shaped organelles. Mitochondria convert the nutrients that enter the cell into ATP. Your cells use ATP for energy. Because they are the cell's powerhouses, you might think of these organelle as the mighty mitochondria.

The nutrients must be digested before they can be converted into energy by the mitochondria. Digestion is carried out by a group of organelles known as lysosomes. Digestive enzymes are found in lysosomes. Enzymes can sometimes be released into the cell. Because the enzymes kill the cell, lysosomes are known as "suicide bags."

_____

Use Google or your preferred source to help match each term with a definition.

1	nucleus	responsible for chromosome segregation
2	lysosomes	degradation of proteins and cellular waste
3	Golgi Apparatus	protein synthesis
4	Mitochondria	lipid synthesis
5	SER	site of photosynthesis
6	RER	stores water in plant cells
7	Microtubules	prevents excessive uptake of water, protects the cell (in plants)
8	ribosomes	degradation of H_2O_2
9	peroxysomes	powerhouse of the cell
10	cell wall	modification of proteins; "post-office" of the cell
11	chloroplast	protein synthesis + modifications
12	central vacuole	where DNA is stored

4th Grade Science: Water Cycle

On stormy days, water falls to the earth. The ground absorbs it. The movement of water is a component of the water cycle. The water cycle is critical to all living things on the planet!

Other cycles exist in your life. Your daily routine is a cycle that begins with you waking up. You attend classes. You take the bus back home. You leave for soccer practice. You eat your dinner. You retire to your bed. These occurrences are part of a cycle. Every weekday, this cycle is repeated. The water cycle is also a series of repeated events that occur repeatedly.

The water cycle is comprised of repeated events such as evaporation, condensation, precipitation, and collection. These occurrences occur regularly.

- Evaporation occurs when water is heated and turns into a gas.
- Condensation occurs when a gas of water cools and condenses back into a liquid.
- Precipitation occurs when water returns to the earth.
- Water is collected when stored in bodies of water such as lakes, rivers, oceans, soil, and rocks.

Observing the water cycle is a good way to see how water moves around the Earth and atmosphere on a daily basis. It is a complicated system with numerous processes. Liquid water evaporates into water vapor, condenses into clouds, and falls back to earth as rain and snow. Water in various phases circulates through the atmosphere (transportation). Runoff is the movement of liquid water across land, into the ground (infiltration and percolation), and through the ground (groundwater). Groundwater moves into plants (plant uptake) and evaporates into the atmosphere from plants (transpiration). Solid ice and snow can spontaneously decompose into gas (sublimation). When water vapor solidifies, the opposite can occur (deposition).

_____

Use the word bank to unscramble the words below.

molecule	pollutant	evaporation	radiation	groundwater	oceans
infiltration	nitrogen	deposition	environment	collection	sublimation
transpiration	hydrogen	condensation	organism	precipitation	oxygen
meltwater	movement	vapor	droplet	iceberg	weather
rainwater	glacier				

. NMSALIITBOU   s u _ l _ _ _ _ _ _ _

. IARTASRPONTIN   _ r _ _ _ _ _ _ _ _ i _ n

. OMLLECUE   _ o _ e _ _ _ _

. NEIRAVOTAOP   _ v _ _ _ _ a _ i _ _

. ALEIGCR   _ l _ _ _ _ r

6. TONOINSNCEDA   c _ _ _ _ n s _ _ _ _

7. DARRWOGENTU   _ r o _ _ _ _ _ _ _ r

8. TUNLOPLAT   _ _ _ l _ _ n _

9. EPITITARINCPO   _ _ _ c _ _ _ t _ _ i _ _

10. ITNIOILRNFAT   _ n _ _ t _ _ _ _ o _

11. ODRLPET   _ r _ _ _ e _

12. NIEDTSOPIO   _ _ _ o _ _ t i _ _

13. WTAEERH   _ _ _ _ h _ r

14. EONNTIGR   n _ _ _ o _ _ _

15. RWANTREAI   r _ _ _ _ _ _ _ r

16. REBGICE   i _ e _ _ _ _

17. TNOAIADRI   _ _ _ _ a _ i _ _

18. EOXNGY   _ x y _ _ _

19. SGOMRNIA   _ _ g _ _ _ _ m

20. YNEDRHOG   _ _ _ r o _ _ _

21. EARTLWTME   _ _ _ _ _ a _ e _

22. COTNCLEOLI   _ o _ _ e _ t _ _ _

23. PAROV   v _ _ _ _

24. NEVOEMTM   _ _ _ _ _ e _ t

25. ORENINTNVEM   e n v _ _ _ _ _ _ _ _

26. OCSANE   _ c _ _ n _

Extra Credit: What is the process of the water cycle?

....

....

....

....

4th Grade Science: The Seasons

Score: _____

Date: _____

First, read the entire passage. After that, go back and fill in the blanks. You can skip the blanks you're unsure about and finish them later.

planet	leaves	North	chicks	green
summer	shines	June	heats	frost

Our _____ has four seasons each year: autumn, winter, spring, and _____.

The Earth spins in a slightly tilted position as it orbits the sun (on an axis tilted 23.5 degrees from a straight-up, vertical position). Because different parts of the planet are angled towards or away from the sun's light throughout the year, this it causes our seasons. More or less sunlight and heat influence the length of each day, the average daily temperature, and the amount of rainfall in different seasons.

The tilt has two major effects: the sun's angle to the Earth and the length of the days. The Earth is tilted so that the _____ Pole is more pointed towards the sun for half of the year. The South Pole is pointing at the sun for the other half. When the North Pole is angled toward the sun, the days in the northern hemisphere (north of the equator) receive more sunlight, resulting in longer days and shorter nights. The northern hemisphere _____ up and experiences summer as the days lengthen. As the year progresses, the Earth's tilt shifts to the North Pole points away from the sun, resulting in winter.

As a result, seasons north of the equator are opposed to seasons south of the equator. When Europe and the United States are experiencing winter, Brazil and Australia will be experiencing summer.

We discussed how the length of the day changes, but the angle of the sun also changes. In the summer, the sun _____ more directly on the Earth, providing more energy to the surface and heating it. In the winter, sunlight strikes the Earth at an angle. This produces less energy and heats the Earthless.

The longest day in the Northern Hemisphere is _____ 21st, while the longest night is December 21st. The opposite is true in the Southern Hemisphere, where December 21st is the longest day, and June 21st is the longest night. There are only two days a year when the day and night are the same. These are September 22nd and March 21st.

The amount of time it is light for decreases in autumn, and the _____ begin to change color and fall off the trees. In the United States of America, autumn is referred to as Fall.

Winter brings colder weather, sometimes snow and _____, no leaves on the trees, and the amount of daylight during the day are at its shortest.

The weather usually warms up in the spring, trees begin to sprout leaves, plants begin to bloom, and young animals such as _____ and lambs are born.

The weather is usually warm in the summer, the trees have entire _____ leaves, and the amount of daylight during the day is extended.

4th Grade History: United States Armed Forces

The President of the United States is the Commander in Chief of the United States Armed Forces.

The United States, like many other countries, maintains a military to safeguard its borders and interests. The military has played an essential role in the formation and history of the United States since the Revolutionary War.

The **United States Department of Defense** (DoD) is in charge of controlling each branch of the military, except the United States Coast Guard, which is under the control of the Department of Homeland Security.

The Department of Defense is the world's largest 'company,' employing over 2 million civilians and military personnel.

The United States military is divided into six branches: the Air Force, Army, Coast Guard, Marine Corps, Navy, and Space Force.

The mission of the **United States Air Force** is to defend the country from outside forces. They also provide air support to other branches of the military, such as the Army and Navy.

The **United States Army** is responsible for defending against aggression that threatens the peace and security of the United States.

There are **Army National Guard** units in all 50 states, which their respective governments govern. The Constitution requires only one branch of the military. Members of the National Guard volunteer some of their time to keep the peace. They are not full-time soldiers, but they respond when called upon, for example, to quell violence when the police need assistance.

The primary concern of **the United States Coast Guard** is to protect domestic waterways (lakes, rivers, ports, etc.). The Coast Guard is managed by the United States Department of Homeland Security.

The **Marines** are a quick-response force. They are prepared to fight on both land and sea. The Marine Corps is a branch of the United States Navy. The Marine Corps conducts operations onboard warfare ships all over the world.

The **United States Navy** conducts its missions at sea to secure and protect the world's oceans. Their mission is to ensure safe sea travel and trade.

The **United States Space Force** is the newest branch of the military, established in December 2019. The world's first and currently only independent space force. It is in charge of operating and defending military satellites and ground stations that provide communications, navigation, and Earth observation, such as missile launch detection.

1. **The United States military is divided into ___ branches.**
   a. six
   b. five

2. **_____ is managed by the United States Department of Homeland Security.**
   a. The National Guard
   b. The Coast Guard

3. **The _____ of the United States is the Commander in Chief of the United States Armed Forces.**
   a. Governor
   b. President

4. **The United States maintains a military to safeguard its _____ and interests.**
   a. borders
   b. cities

5. **DoD is in charge of controlling each _____of the military.**
   a. branch
   b. army

6. **The Marines are prepared to fight on both land and ____.**
   a. battlefield
   b. sea

7. **The United States Space Force is in charge of operating and defending military ____ and ground stations.**
   a. soldiers
   b. satellites

8. **The mission of the _____ is to defend the country from outside forces.**
   a. United States DoD Forces
   b. United States Air Force

9. **There are _____ units in all 50 states.**
   a. Army National Guard
   b. Armed Nations Guard

10. **The United States Navy conducts its missions at sea to secure and protect the world's _____.**
    a. oceans
    b. borders

11. **The primary concern of the United States Coast Guard is to protect_____.**
    a. domestic waterways
    b. domesticated cities

12. **The United States military is: the Amy Force, Army, Coast Guard, Mario Corps, Old Navy, and Space Force.**
    a. True
    b. False

xtra Credit: Has America ever been invaded?

4th Grade Government History:
How Laws Are Made

Congress is the federal government's legislative branch, and it is in charge of making laws for the entire country. Congress is divided into two legislative chambers: the United States Senate and the United States House of Representatives. Anyone elected to either body has the authority to propose new legislation. A bill is a new law proposal.

People living in the United States and its territories are subject to federal laws.

Bills are created and passed by Congress. The president may then sign the bills into law. Federal courts may examine the laws to see if they are in accordance with the Constitution. If a court finds a law to be unconstitutional, it has the authority to overturn it.

The United States government has enacted several laws to help maintain order and protect the country's people. Each new law must be approved by both houses of Congress as well as the President. Before it becomes a new law in the nation, each law must go through a specific process.

The majority of laws in the United States begin as bills. An idea is the starting point for a bill. That thought could come from anyone, including you. The idea must then be written down and explained as the next step. A bill is the name given to the first draft of an idea. The bill must then be sponsored by a member of Congress. The sponsor is someone who strongly supports the bill and wishes to see it become law. A Senator or a member of the House of Representatives can be the sponsor.

The bill is then introduced in either the House or the Senate by the bill's sponsor. Once submitted, the bill is given a number and is officially recorded as a bill.

The bill is assigned to a committee after it is introduced. Committees are smaller groups of congress members who are experts in specific areas. For example, if the bill concerns classroom size in public schools, it would be referred to the Committee on Education. The committee goes over the bill's specifics. They bring in experts from outside Congress to testify and debate the bill's pros and cons.

The committee may decide to make changes to the bill before it is passed. If the committee finally agrees to pass the bill, it will be sent to the House or Senate's main chamber for approval.

If the bill was introduced in the House, it would first be considered by the House. The bill will be discussed and debated by the representatives. House members will then vote on the bill. If the bill is passed, it will be sent to the Senate for consideration.

The Senate will then follow the same procedure. It will discuss and debate the bill before voting. If the Senate approves the bill, it will be sent to the President.

The President's signature is the final step in a bill becoming law. When the President signs the bill, it becomes law.

The President has the option of refusing to sign the bill. This is known as a veto. The Senate and House can choose to override the President's veto by voting again. The bill must now be approved by a two-thirds majority in both the Senate and the House to override the veto.

A bill must be signed into law by the President within 10-days. If he does not sign it within 10-days, one of two things may occur:

1) It will become law if Congress is in session.

2) It will be considered vetoed if Congress is not in session (this is called a pocket veto).

1. **If the Senate approves the bill, it will be sent to the _____.**
   a. President
   b. House Representee

2. **The _____ may decide to make changes to the bill before it is passed.**
   a. governor
   b. committee

3. **The bill must then be _____ by a member of Congress.**
   a. signed
   b. sponsored

4. **The President has the option of refusing to sign the bill. This is known as a ___.**
   a. voted
   b. veto

5. **The Senate and House can choose to override the President's veto by _____ again.**
   a. creating a new bill
   b. voting

6. **The bill is assigned to a committee after it is _____.**
   a. introduced
   b. vetoed

7. **Bills are created and passed by _____.**
   a. The House
   b. Congress

8. **A bill must be signed into law by the President within ___-days.**
   a. 10
   b. 5

9. **The President's _____ is the final step in a bill becoming law.**
   a. signature
   b. saying yes

10. **If the committee agrees to pass the bill, it will be sent to the House or Senate's main ___ for approval.**
    a. chamber
    b. state

Extra Credit: What are some of the weirdest laws in the world? List at least 5.

4th Grade History: The Vikings

First, read the entire passage. After that, go back and fill in the blanks. You can skip the blanks you're unsure about and finish them late

sail	settle	North	Christianity	raided
Middle	defeated	shallow	cargo	Denmark

During the _____ Ages, the Vikings lived in Northern Europe. They first settled in the Scandinavian lands that are now Denmark, Sweden, and Norway. During the Middle Ages, the Vikings played a significant role in Northern Europe, particularly during the Viking Age, which lasted from 800 CE to 1066 CE.

In Old Norse, the word Viking means "to raid." The Vikings would board their longships and _____ across the seas to raid villages o Europe's northern coast, including islands like Great Britain. In 787 CE, they first appeared in England to raid villages. When the Vikings _____, they were known to attack defenseless monasteries. This earned them a bad reputation as barbarians, but monasteries were wealthy and undefended Viking targets.

The Vikings eventually began to _____ in areas other than Scandinavia. They colonized parts of Great Britain, Germany, and Iceland in the ninth century. They spread into northeastern Europe, including Russia, in the 10th century. They also established Normandy, which means "Northmen," along the coast of northern France.

By the beginning of the 11th century, the Vikings had reached the pinnacle of their power. Leif Eriksson, son of Erik the Red, was one Viking who made it to _____ America. He established a brief settlement in modern-day Canada. This was thousands of years before Columbus.

The English and King Harold Godwinson _____ the Vikings, led by King Harald Hardrada of Norway, in 1066. The defeat in this battle is sometimes interpreted as the end of the Viking Age. The Vikings stopped expanding their territory at this point, and raids became less frequent.

The arrival of Christianity was a major factor at the end of the Viking age. The Vikings became more and more a part of mainland Europ as Scandinavia was converted to _____ and became a part of Christian Europe. Sweden's, Denmark's, and Norway's identities and borders began to emerge as well.

The Vikings were perhaps best known for their ships. The Vikings built longships for exploration and raiding. Longships were long, narrow vessels built for speed. Oars primarily propelled them but later added a sail to help in windy conditions. Longships had a shallow draft, which allowed them to float in _____ water and land on beaches.

The Vikings also built _____ ships known as Knarr for trading. The Knarr was wider and deeper than the longship, allowing it to transport more cargo.

Five recovered Viking ships can be seen at the Viking Ship Museum in Roskilde, _____. It's also possible to see how the Vikings built their ships. The Vikings used a shipbuilding technique known as clinker building. They used long wood planks that overlapped along the edges.

Fun Facts:

- The Viking is the mascot of the Minnesota Vikings of the National Football League.
- Certain Vikings fought with monstrous two-handed axes. They are capable of easily piercing a metal helmet or shield.

Extra Credit: Do Vikings still exist?

Score: _____

Date: _____

4th Grade Science: Coral Reefs

First, read the entire passage. After that, go back and fill in the blanks. You can skip the blanks you're unsure about and finish them later.

biomes	rocks	Photosynthesis	Barrier	25%
living	harden	shallow	habitation	atoll
Fringe	survive	Australia	Great	algae

One of the most important marine _____ is the coral reef. Coral reefs are home to approximately _____ of all known marine species, despite being a relatively small biome.

Coral reefs may appear to be made of _____ at first glance, but they are actually _____ organisms. These organisms are polyps, which are tiny little animals. Polyps live on the reef's periphery. When polyps die, they _____ and new polyps grow on top of them, causing the reef to expand.

Because polyps must eat to _____, you can think of the coral reef as eating as well. They eat plankton and _____, which are small animals. _____ is how algae get their food from the sun. This is why coral reefs form near the water's surface and in clear water where the algae can be fed by the sun.

To form, coral reefs require warm, _____ water. They form near the equator, near coastlines, and around islands all over the world. Southeast Asia and the region around _____ are home to a sizable portion of the world's coral reefs. The Great Barrier Reef, located off the coast of Queensland, Australia, is the world's largest coral reef. The _____ Barrier Reef is 2,600 miles long.

Coral reefs are classified into three types:

_____ reefs are reefs that grow close to the shore. It may be attached to the shore, or there may be a narrow swath of water known as a lagoon or channel between the land and the coral reef.

_____ reef - Barrier reefs grow away from the shoreline, sometimes for several miles.

An _____ is a coral ring that surrounds a lagoon of water. It begins as a fringe reef surrounding a volcanic island. As the coral grows, the island sinks into the ocean, leaving only the coral ring. Some atolls are large enough to support human _____. The Maldives is an example of this.

4th Grade Storytime Reading:
The Wolf & 7 Kids

Hello Friend! You're going to read a story that's **not** real; it is fiction. Fiction is any story made up by an author. It is a creation of the author's imagination.

First, read the entire passage. After that, go back and fill in the blanks. You can skip the blanks you're unsure about and finish them last.

poor	terrified	table	good	snoring
rose	scissors	swallowed	dashed	returned
hunger	knocked	inserted	rattled	paws
forest	wide	mother	stomach	water

The story goes that once upon a time, an old Goat had seven little Kids and adored them with all the affection a _____ would have for her children.

She wanted to go into the _____ and get some food one day. So she called up all seven children to her and said, "Dear Children, I must go into the forest." Keep an eye out for the Wolf. If he gets in, he'll eat your whole skin, hair, and all. The wretch frequently disguises himself, but you'll recognize him right away by his rough voice and black feet."

"Dear Mother, we will take _____ care of ourselves," the children said. You may leave without wariness."

The old one bleated and went on her way, her mind at ease.

It wasn't long before someone _____ on the door and yelled, "Open the door, dear Children! Your mother has arrived, and she has brought something for each of you."

The little Kids, however, recognized the Wolf by his rough voice. "We will not open the door," they cried, "because you are not our mother." Your voice is rough, whereas hers is soft and pleasant. "You are Wolf!"

The Wolf then went to a shopkeeper and bought a large lump of chalk, which he ate and used to soften his voice. Then he returned, knocked on the door, and cried, "Open the door, dear Children! Your mother has arrived and has brought something for each of you."

However, the Wolf had placed his black _____ against the window, and when the children saw them, they cried out, "We will not open the door; our mother does not have black feet like you." "You are Wolf!"

The Wolf then _____ over to a baker and said, "I've hurt my feet; rub some dough over them for me."

After rubbing his feet, the baker ran to the miller and said, "Strew some white meal over my feet for me." "The Wolf wants to deceive someone," the miller reasoned, and he refused. "If you don't do it," the Wolf said, "I will devour you." The miller became _____ and whitened his paws for him. Yes, and so are men!

Now, for the third time, the wretch went to the house-door, knocked, and said, "Open the door for me, Children!" Your dear little mother has _____ home, and she has brought something from the forest for each of you."

"First show us your paws so we can tell if you are our dear little mother," the children cried.

Then he _____ his paws through the window. When the kids saw they were white, they believed everything he said and opened the door. But who else but the Wolf should enter?

They were terrified and wished to remain hidden. One jumped under the _____, another into the bed, a third into the stove, a four into the kitchen, a fifth into the cupboard, a sixth into the washing bowl, and a seventh into the clock case. But the Wolf found them all and _____ them down his throat one after the other. The only one he didn't find was the youngest in the clock case.

When the Wolf had satisfied his _____, he exited the building, sat down under a tree in the green meadow outside, and fell asleep.

Soon after, the old Goat returned from the forest. What a sight she saw over there! The front door was _____ open. The table, chairs, and benches were thrown to the ground, the washing bowl was shattered, and the quilts and pillows were yanked from the bed.

She went looking for her children, but they were nowhere to be found. She called out their names one by one, but no one answered. When she finally summoned the youngest, a soft voice cried out, "Dear Mother, I am in the clock-case."

She took the Kid out, and it informed her that the Wolf had arrived and devoured all the others. You can only imagine how she cried over her _____ children!

In her grief, she eventually went out, and the youngest Kid followed her. When they arrived at the meadow, the Wolf by the tree was _____ so loudly that the branches shook. She examined him from every angle and noticed that something was moving and struggling in his stomach. "Ah!" she exclaimed, "is it possible that my poor children, whom he has devoured for his supper, are still alive?"

The Kid then had to dash home to get _____, a needle and thread, and the Goat to cut open the monster's stomach. She had barely made one cut when a little Kid thrust its head out, and when she had cut further, all six sprang out one after the other, all still alive and unharmed, because the monster had swallowed them whole in his greed.

There was a lot of joy! They ran up to their mother and jumped like a tailor at his wedding. "Now go and look for some big stones," the mother said. We'll stuff them into the wicked beast's _____ while he's sleeping."

The seven Kids then dragged the stones with all haste, stuffing as many as they could into his stomach. And the mother sewed him up again in haste so that he was unaware of anything and never moved.

When the Wolf awoke from his slumber, he _____ to his feet, and because the stones in his stomach were making him thirsty, he desired to go to a well to drink. When he started walking and moving around, the stones in his stomach knocked against each other and _____. Then he cried out:

"What is it that rumbles and tumbles Against my poor bones?"
I thought it was six children, but it's just big stones!"

And as he approached the well, stooped over the _____, and was about to drink, the heavy stones caused him to fall in. There was no way to save him, so he had to drown!

When the seven Kids saw this, they dashed to the spot and exclaimed, "The Wolf is dead! "The Wolf has died!" and joyfully danced around the well with their mother.

4th Grade Spelling Words

Use the word bank to unscramble the words below.

bubble	community	reject	husband	pineapple	hostile
compass	tomatoes	alarm	salute	perhaps	fugitive
friends	council	fountain	goose	ankle	tutor
difference	center	hammer	jewel	choir	fatal
children	subject				

. RNIEFDS   _ _ i _ n _ _

. UGITIFVE   f _ g _ _ _ _ _

. EPLIPPNAE   _ _ n _ _ _ _ _ e

. RSEPAPH   _ _ r _ _ p _

. COIRH   _ _ o _ _

. AOTFNUIN   _ o u _ _ _ _ _

. EGOSO   _ _ _ s _

. ERAMMH   h a _ _ _ _

. LOCNUIC   _ _ u _ _ i _

0. LHOTEIS   _ o _ _ _ _ e

1. AALTF   _ _ _ a _

2. JLEWE   _ _ w _ _

3. CTIMMUNOY   _ _ _ m _ _ _ t _

14. ASCMPOS   _ _ _ _ a _ s

15. LASUTE   _ _ l _ _ e

16. ESTUCJB   _ _ _ j _ c _

17. CLEDHNRI   _ _ _ _ _ _ r e _

18. RCEEJT   _ e _ e _ _

19. CIDFEFREEN   _ i f _ _ _ _ _ c _

20. NLEAK   _ _ _ l _

21. HANDSUB   _ u s _ _ _ _

22. EECRTN   _ e _ t _ _

23. MOSOTAET   _ o _ a _ _ _ _

24. OURTT   _ _ _ _ r

25. RALMA   _ _ _ r _

26. LEBUBB   b _ _ b _ _

4th Grade Grammar: Sentence Building

Practice *sentence* building. U*nscramble* the words to form a complete sentence.

1. _____ can build _____ ___ _____ _____ _____
   antibiotics. · up · Germs · to · a · resistance

2. _____ _____ a _____ _____ _____ the _____
   in · curve · road. · There · was · sharp

3. Let's _____ ___ graph _____ _____ _____
   make · this · a · with · data.

4. ___ like _____ _____ _____ _____ _____ potatoes.
   turkey · mashed · to · eat · and · I

5. _____ _____ built a _____ _____ _____ _____
   clay. · of · out · house · sister · My

6. _____ flight _____ very _____ _____ _____
   boring. · The · was · long · and

7. ___ heard _____ _____ _____ very _____
   wealthy. · that · man · is · I

8. ___ will _____ _____ _____ _____ for _____
   soup · have · I · and · lunch. · crackers

9. There _____ ___ _____ behind _____ _____
   my · brook · home. · a · is

10. ___ _____ to _____ _____
    I · like · water. · drink

11. How _____ _____ _____ _____ this _____
    sickness? · you · had · have · long

12. ____ _____ _____ books _____ elephants.
    many · wrote · about · He

13. ____ _____ _____ ____ normal.
    temperature · is · My · body

14. __ have __ _____ _____ sometimes.
    weak · a · I · stomach

15. _____ _____ while __ _____ your _____
    Stay · still · fix · I · tie.

16. ____ _____ _____ ____ _____ this morning.
    started · to · My · ache · head

17. ____ _____ _____ _____ ____ an office.
    My · works · big · in · brother

18. _____ _____ cars _____ _____ forward.
    train · The · kept · lurching

19. __ can't possibly _____ __ _____
    prediction. · a · I · make

20. __ _____ my school _____ _____ _____
    I · like · picture · this · year.

21. _____ _____ pizza have _____ ____ _____
    the · it? · Will · on · everything

22. ____ _____ ____ _____ dear to _____
    My · is · cat · me. · very

23. I _____ a _____ _____ ____ _____
    want · not · enemy. · friend, · an

24. _____ _____ guess ____ _____
    my · you · Can · weight?

4th Grade Geography: Castles in Germany

Castles are now iconic symbols of magnificence and mythical tales. Aside from their dazzling appearance and antiquity, they reveal an old vivid, and true fable.

German castles date from the 9th to 10th centuries, when the Great Age of Castles began. Castles embody the need for nations to be protected from invasions by other countries and serve as residences for old royal families. These incredible structures are examples of tactical and solid rocky constructions built by kings and emperors to guard the nation's territories during warfare and impose rule among populaces during peacetime.

German castles evolved during the "Medieval Ages," following the fall of Ancient Rome and the beginning of the Renaissance Period in the 14th century, and are considered an area of art and architecture. The architecture of German castles consists of a combination of towers and fortified walls, with amazingly decorated interior and exterior, located in high peaks of mountains and valleys, near waterways, and allowing total surveillance of the surrounding territory.

Modern Germany has a magnificent castle heritage, with over 2100 castles spread throughout the country. A very bright and amusing history awaits behind the doors of these impressive castles. Around 100 years ago, not so long ago, kings, emperors, and their families visited, lived, and operated there. Historical resolutions were reached there, and many soldiers died there defending their country from invaders.

Let us take some time to explore some of Germany's magnificent castles.

Neuschwanstein Castle: Located in the Bavarian Alps near the town of Füssen in southeast Bavaria, Germany, this is one of Europe's and the world's most impressive castles.

Hohenzollern Castle is situated on the crest of Mount Hohenzollern in the German state of Swabia. It was first built in the 11th century.

Eltz Castle: The beautiful and ancient castle of Eltz is located in the Moselle valley, between Koblenz and Trier, Germany, and is surrounded on three sides by the Eltzbach River. The castle was built as a residence rather than a fortress and served as a residence for the Rodendorf, Kempenich, and Rübenach families.

Heidelberg Castle: Heidelberg Castle (German: *Heidelberger Schloss*) is unquestionably Germany's most famous castle ruin. The magnificent palace commands a commanding position on a hill overlooking historic Heidelberg. Schloss Heidelberg has inspired poets for centuries, so it's no surprise that it's a popular tourist destination and well-known worldwide.

Schwerin Castle: Schwerin Castle is located in the city of Schwerin, Germany. Schwerin Castle is now the seat of the local government and an art museum displaying works from antiquity to the twentieth century. The museum's seventeenth-century Dutch and Flemish paintings are among its most important exhibits.

1. _____ is now the seat of the local government and an art museum.
   a. Schwerin Castle
   b. Swaziland Castle

2. Hohenzollern Castle is situated on the _____ of Mount Hohenzollern.
   a. crest
   b. end

3. The architecture of German castles consists of a combination of towers and _____.
   a. beautiful curtains
   b. fortified walls

4. German castles evolved during the "_____ Ages".
   a. Century
   b. Medieval

5. This castle was built as a residence rather than a fortress.
   a. Eltz Castle
   b. Schwerin Castle

6. Castles are now iconic symbols of magnificence and _____ tales.
   a. real life
   b. mythical

7. _____has inspired poets for centuries.
   a. Schloss Heidelberg
   b. Steven Spielberg

8. _____Castle is located in the Bavarian Alps near the town of Füssen.
   a. Norwegian
   b. Neuschwanstein

4th Grade Geography
Vocabulary Crossword

Complete the crossword by filling in a word that fits each clue. Fill in the correct answers, one letter per square, both across and down, from the given clues. There will be a gray space between multi-word answers.

Tip: Solve the easy clues first, and then go back and answer the more difficult ones.

Across

1. a bowl-shaped vessel used for holding food or liquids
9. water that has condensed on a cool surface overnight
10. droplets of water vapor suspended in the air near the ground
11. ice crystals forming a white deposit
12. a slowly moving mass of ice
16. a shelter serving as a place of safety or sanctuary
17. a relatively flat highland
18. an extensive plain without trees
20. topographic study of a given place
21. a long steep-sided depression in the ocean floor
23. A circular, spiral, or helical motion in a fluid
24. a low area where the land is saturated with water

Down

2. an indentation of a shoreline smaller than a gulf
3. a large cave or a large chamber in a cave
4. a steep rock face
5. the shore of a sea or ocean
6. the territory occupied by a nation
7. an open valley in a hilly area
8. arid land with little or no vegetation
13. precipitation of ice pellets
14. a large frozen mass floating at sea
15. a thin fog with condensation near the ground
18. air pollution by a mixture of smoke and fog
23. a valley
25. a slight wind

GLACIER   ZEPHYR   ICEBERG
DESERT   FROST   DALE   HAIL
SMOG   BASIN   VALE   BAY
OASIS   COUNTRY   COAST
TOPOLOGY   WETLAND   MIST
STEPPE   VORTEX   PLATEAU
FOG   DEW   CLIFF   TRENCH
CAVERN

4th Grade Geography: Canada

Score: _____

Date: _____

Canada is the world's second-largest country, covering 10 million square kilometers. Canada's borders are bounded by three oceans: the Pacific Ocean to the west, the Atlantic Ocean to the east, and the Arctic Ocean to the north. The Canada-United States border runs along Canada's southern border.

Queen Victoria, Queen Elizabeth II's great-great-grandmother, chose Ottawa, which is located on the Ottawa River, as the capital in 1857. It is now the fourth largest metropolitan area in Canada. The National Capital Region, which encompasses 4,700 square kilometers around Ottawa, preserves and improves the area's built heritage and natural environment.

Canada is divided into ten provinces and three territories. Each province and territory has a separate capital city. You should be familiar with the capitals of your province or territory, as well as those of Canada.

Below are some of Canada's Territories, Provinces, and Capital Cities. Draw a line through each word you find.

```
R   L   U   G   M   A   N   I   T   O   B   A   N   K   M   E   X   L   S   P
W   K   A   K   B   B   H   A   L   B   E   R   T   A   G   D   K   P   R   R
Q   M   N   Y   N   X   W   I   S   Z   L   X   B   Q   E   K   B   T   X   I
I   Q   A   L   U   I   T   E   G   I   R   T   O   R   O   N   T   O   Y   N
A   B   R   I   T   I   S   H   C   O   L   U   M   B   I   A   E   C   E   C
V   N   N   R   S   Q   H   G   I   W   I   N   N   I   P   E   G   H   L   E
S   O   G   X   Z   G   A   O   N   T   A   R   I   O   F   B   R   A   L   E
T   V   Q   Z   E   D   M   O   N   T   O   N   C   D   F   W   Q   R   O   D
.   A   V   H   B   E   F   R   E   D   E   R   I   C   T   O   N   L   W   W
J   S   V   P   O   Q   U   E   B   E   C   C   I   T   Y   N   W   O   K   A
O   C   Y   J   R   W   S   H   V   C   V   Q   H   W   W   U   L   T   N   R
H   O   E   L   E   E   B   A   A   Z   O   U   Q   G   H   N   V   T   I   D
N   T   W   X   G   A   Q   L   S   T   J   E   F   H   I   A   I   E   F   I
'   I   K   M   I   D   C   I   I   X   L   B   U   V   T   V   C   T   E   S
S   A   C   P   N   C   O   F   T   Z   M   E   U   E   E   U   T   O   N   L
P   Q   Y   F   A   P   L   A   G   P   Y   C   F   M   H   T   O   W   B   A
I   W   S   D   R   Y   W   X   G   W   P   U   E   U   O   G   R   N   M   N
Y   N   E   W   B   R   U   N   S   W   I   C   K   T   R   P   I   C   R   D
R   X   B   T   E   R   V   Y   J   B   H   H   M   K   S   W   A   J   N   Z
G   F   S   A   S   K   A   T   C   H   E   W   A   N   E   Y   U   K   O   N
```

Yukon	Nunavut	Nova Scotia	Prince Edward Island	New Brunswick
Quebec	Ontario	Manitoba	Saskatchewan	Alberta
British Columbia	Victoria	Edmonton	Regina	Winnipeg
Toronto	Quebec City	Fredericton	Charlottetown	Halifax
St. John's	Iqaluit	Yellowknife	Whitehorse	

4th Grade Art: Draw Facial Expressions

Facial expressions are one of the most effective ways for humans to communicate with one another. We learn to distinguish between a happy and an angry expression from a very young age. As we get older, we develop the ability to express our feelings and read other people's thoughts and emotions without using words.

Try looking at photos of yourself or others expressing various emotions and studying them to identify which parts of your face are moving. It is a great way to start learning how to draw facial expressions and understand points of tension. The more intense the emotion, the more areas of the face are involved.

4th Grade Art: Finish The Pictures & Color

Finish the picture

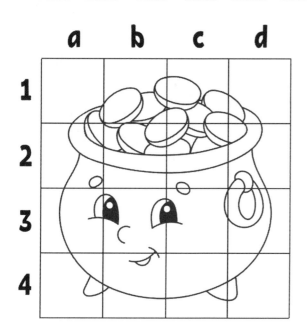

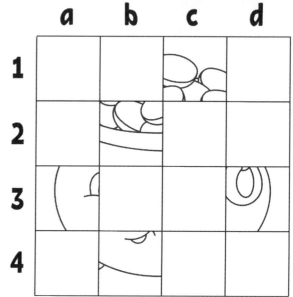

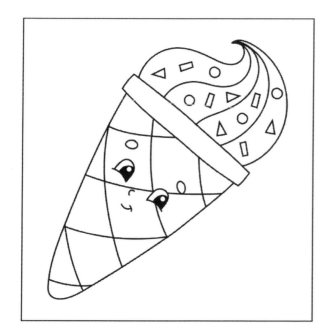

4th Grade Music: Instruments

Music is a type of art derived from the Greek word for "art of the Muses." The Muses were the goddesses of ancient Greece who inspired the arts such as literature, music, and poetry.

Music has been performed with instruments and through vocal songs since the dawn of time. While it is unknown how or when the first musical instrument was created, most historians point to at least 37,000-year-old flutes made from animal bones. The oldest known written song is 4,000 years old and was written in ancient cuneiform.

Instruments were created in order to produce musical sounds. Any object that produces sound, especially if it was designed for that purpose, can be considered a musical instrument.

P	T	R	O	M	B	O	N	E	X	I	X
O	I	C	L	A	R	I	N	E	T	D	B
R	B	A	B	A	S	S	O	O	N	R	C
E	A	O	N	B	I	Q	Q	P	J	U	U
C	F	Q	E	O	Y	E	Z	I	S	M	Z
O	W	O	O	D	B	L	O	C	K	S	O
R	S	A	X	O	P	H	O	N	E	Z	R
D	K	E	T	R	U	M	P	E	T	O	G
E	Z	A	Y	J	F	L	U	T	E	I	A
R	F	R	E	N	C	H	H	O	R	N	N
F	O	Y	R	X	A	H	S	J	R	I	I
G	U	I	T	A	R	V	I	O	L	I	N

PIANO	FLUTE	BASSOON	CLARINET	TROMBONE
VIOLIN	WOODBLOCK	TRUMPET	OBOE	SAXOPHONE
GUITAR	DRUMS	ORGAN	RECORDER	FRENCH HORN

4th Grade Music: Musical Terms

Complete the crossword by filling in a word that fits each clue. Fill in the correct answers, one letter per square, both across and down, from the given clues. There will be a gray space between multi-word answers.

Tip: Solve the easy clues first, and then go back and answer the more difficult ones.

Across

2. the highest adult male singing voice; singing falsetto
4. the part of a song that transitions between two main parts
5. a combination of three or more tones sounded simultaneously
8. making up the song or melody as you play
11. a song written for one or more instruments playing solo
12. the highest of the singing voices
13. is a poem set to music with a recurring pattern of both rhyme and meter
14. timing or speed of the music

Down

1. singing without any instruments
3. low, the lowest of the voices and the lowest part of the harmony
6. to play a piece of music sweetly, tender, adoring manner
7. the sound of two or more notes heard simultaneously
9. is a musical interval; the distance between one note
10. played by a single musical instrument or voice
15. a range of voice that is between the bass and the alto
16. the repeating changing of the pitch of a note

CHORD   BRIDGE   ALTO
HARMONY   SOPRANO
IMPROVISATION   DOLCE
OCTAVE   VIBRATO   STANZA
SONATA   A CAPPELLA   TEMPO
BASS   SOLO   TENOR

4th Grade Health: The Food Groups

First, read the entire passage. After that, go back and fill in the blanks. You can skip the blanks you're unsure about and finish them later.

produce	consume	yogurt	stored	bones
repair	water	portion	vitamins	fiber

Eating healthy foods is especially important for children because they are still developing. Children's bodies require nutrition to develop strong, healthy _____ and muscles. You will not grow as tall or as strong as you could if you do not get all the _____ and minerals you require while growing.

Healthy food includes a wide variety of fresh foods from the five healthy food groups:

Dairy: Milk, cheese, and _____ are the most critical dairy foods, which are necessary for strong and healthy bones. There aren't many other foods in our diet that have as much calcium as these.

Fruit: Fruit contains vitamins, minerals, dietary fiber, and various phytonutrients (nutrients found naturally in plants) that help your body stay healthy. Fruits and vegetables provide you with energy, antioxidants, and _____. These nutrients help protect you against diseases later in life, such as heart disease, stroke, and some cancers.

Vegetables and legumes/beans: Vegetables should account for a large _____ of your daily food intake and should be encouraged at all meals (including snack times). To keep your body healthy, they supply vitamins, minerals, dietary fiber, and phytonutrients (nutrients found naturally in plants).

Grain (cereal) foods: choose wholegrain and/or high _____ bread, cereals, rice, pasta, noodles, and so on. These foods provide you with the energy you require to grow, develop, and learn. Refined grain products (such as cakes and biscuits) can contain added sugar, fat, and sodium.

Protein from lean meats and poultry, fish, eggs, tofu, nuts and seeds, and legumes/beans is used by our bodies to _____ specialized chemicals such as hemoglobin and adrenalin. Protein also helps to build, maintain, and _____ tissues in our bodies. Protein is the primary component of muscles and organs (such as your heart).

Calories are a unit of measurement for the amount of energy in food. We gain calories when we eat, which gives us the energy to run around and do things. If we _____ more calories than we expend while moving, our bodies will store the excess calories as fat. If we burn more calories than we consume, our bodies will begin to burn the previously _____ fat.

Consider the five food groups when making your grocery list: fruits, vegetables, grains, protein foods, and dairy or fortified soy alternatives. Examine the foods you already have in your refrigerator, freezer, and pantry, and then go shopping for any items you may be missing.

See if you can create a grocery list for each of the five food groups.

Grocery List

Fruits & Veggies
- ☐ potatoes
- ☐ tomatoes
- ☐ _____
- ☐ _____

Refrigerated
- ☐ butter
- ☐ cheese
- ☐ eggs
- ☐ milk
- ☐ _____

Frozen
- ☐ _____
- ☐ _____
- ☐ _____

Packages
- ☐ cereal
- ☐ pasta
- ☐ rice
- ☐ soup
- ☐ _____
- ☐ _____

Baking & Bread
- ☐ bread
- ☐ flour
- ☐ sugar
- ☐ _____
- ☐ _____

Miscellaneous
- ☐ paper towels
- ☐ soap
- ☐ toothpaste
- ☐ _____
- ☐ _____

Grocery List

Fruits & Veggies
- ☐ potatoes
- ☐ tomatoes
- ☐ _____
- ☐ _____

Refrigerated
- ☐ butter
- ☐ cheese
- ☐ eggs
- ☐ milk
- ☐ _____

Frozen
- ☐ _____
- ☐ _____
- ☐ _____

Packages
- ☐ cereal
- ☐ pasta
- ☐ rice
- ☐ soup
- ☐ _____
- ☐ _____

Baking & Bread
- ☐ bread
- ☐ flour
- ☐ sugar
- ☐ _____
- ☐ _____

Miscellaneous
- ☐ paper towels
- ☐ soap
- ☐ toothpaste
- ☐ _____
- ☐ _____

Grocery List

Fruits & Veggies
- ☐ potatoes
- ☐ tomatoes
- ☐ _____
- ☐ _____

Refrigerated
- ☐ butter
- ☐ cheese
- ☐ eggs
- ☐ milk
- ☐ _____

Frozen
- ☐ _____
- ☐ _____
- ☐ _____

Packages
- ☐ cereal
- ☐ pasta
- ☐ rice
- ☐ soup
- ☐ _____
- ☐ _____

Baking & Bread
- ☐ bread
- ☐ flour
- ☐ sugar
- ☐ _____
- ☐ _____

Miscellaneous
- ☐ paper towels
- ☐ soap
- ☐ toothpaste
- ☐ _____
- ☐ _____

4th Grade Environmental Health: Water Pollution

First, read the entire passage. After that, go back and fill in the blanks. You can skip the blanks you're unsure about and finish them later.

naturally	spills	toxic	crops	causes
streams	Gulf	wastewater	Acid	ill

Water pollution occurs when waste, chemicals, or other particles cause a body of water (e.g., rivers, oceans, lakes) to become _____ to the fish and animals that rely on it for survival. Water pollution can also disrupt and hurt nature's water cycle.

Water pollution can occur _____ due to volcanoes, algae blooms, animal waste, and silt from storms and floods.

Human activity contributes significantly to water pollution. Sewage, pesticides, fertilizers from farms, wastewater and chemicals from factories, silt from construction sites, and trash from people littering are some human _____.

Oil _____ have been some of the most well-known examples of water pollution. The Exxon Valdez oil spill occurred when an oil tanker collided with a reef off the coast of Alaska, causing over 11 million gallons of oil to spill into the ocean. Another major oil spill was the Deepwater Horizon oil spill, which occurred when an oil well exploded, causing over 200 million gallons of oil to spill into the _____ of Mexico.

Water pollution can be caused directly by air pollution. When sulfur dioxide particles reach high altitudes in the atmosphere, they can combine with rain to form acid rain. _____ rain can cause lakes to become acidic, killing fish and other animals.

The main issue caused by water pollution is the impact on aquatic life. Dead fish, birds, dolphins, and various other animals frequently wash up on beaches, killed by pollutants in their environment. Pollution also has an impact on the natural food chain. Small animals consume contaminants like lead and cadmium.

Clean water is one of the most valuable and essential commodities for life on Earth. Clean water is nearly impossible to obtain for over 1 billion people on the planet. They can become _____ from dirty, polluted water, which is especially difficult for young children. Some bacteria and pathogens in water can make people sick to the point of death.

Water pollution comes from a variety of sources. Here are a few of the main reasons:

Sewage: In many parts of the world, sewage is still flushed directly into _____ and rivers. Sewage can produce dangerous bacteria that can make humans and animals very sick.

Farm animal waste: Runoff from large herds of farm animals such as pigs and cows can enter the water supply due to rain and large storms.

Pesticides: Pesticides and herbicides are frequently sprayed on _____ to kill bugs, while herbicides are sprayed to kill weeds. These potent chemicals can enter the water through rainstorm runoff. They can also contaminate rivers and lakes due to unintentional spills.

Construction, floods, and storms: Silt from construction, earthquakes, and storms can reduce water oxygen levels and suffocate fish.

Factories: Water is frequently used in factories to process chemicals, keep engines cool, and wash things away. Sometimes used _____ is dumped into rivers or the ocean. It may contain pollutants.

4th Grade: Weather and Climate

The difference between weather and climate is simply a matter of time. Weather refers to the conditions of the atmosphere over a short period of time, whereas climate refers to how the atmosphere "behaves" over a longer period of time.

When we discuss climate change, we are referring to changes in long-term averages of daily weather. Today's children are constantly told by their parents and grandparents about how the snow was always piled up to their waists as they trudged off to school. Most children today have not experienced those kinds of dreadful snow-packed winters. The recent changes in winter snowfall indicate that the climate has changed since their parents were children.

Weather is essentially the atmosphere's behavior, particularly in terms of its effects on life and human activities. The distinction between weather and climate is that weather refers to short-term (minutes to months) changes in the atmosphere, whereas climate refers to long-term changes. Most people associate weather with temperature, humidity, precipitation, cloudiness, brightness, visibility, wind, and atmospheric pressure, as in high and low pressure.

Weather can change from minute to minute, hour to hour, day to day, and season to season in most places. However, the climate is the average of weather over time and space. A simple way to remember the distinction is that climate is what you expect, such as a very hot summer, whereas weather is what you get, such as a hot day with pop-up thunderstorms.

Use the word bank to unscramble the words!

Pressure	Density	Cloudy	Latitude	Elevation	Weather
Absorb	Humid	Precipitation	Windy	Forecast	Climate
Sunshine	Temperature				

1. IUMHD   _ u _ _ _

2. UDLOYC   _ l _ u _ _

3. FSEATOCR   _ _ _ _ _ a _ t

4. UDLTITAE   L _ _ _ _ u _ _

5. IEOCAIIPPTRNT   _ _ _ _ _ _ _ t _ _ _ o n

6. TEEERPAURMT   T _ _ _ e _ _ t _ _ _

7. RSEREUPS   _ r e _ _ _ _ _

8. LEICATM   _ _ i _ _ t _

9. SNNIEHUS   S _ _ _ _ _ i _ _

10. OBBASR   _ b s _ _ _

11. VETIEOANL   _ _ _ _ a t _ _ _

12. EATWRHE   W _ _ _ _ e _

13. NDWIY   _ _ _ _ y

14. TYNEIDS   _ _ _ _ i _ y

Cursive Writing Practice

Why did the teacher wear

sunglasses? (Because her

students were bright!) Why

was the teacher cross-eyed?

(She couldn't control her

pupils!) How do bees get to

school? (By school buzz!)

What did the paper say to

the pencil? (Write on!) How

do you get straight As? (Use

Cursive Writing Practice

a ruler!) What building has

the most stories? (The

library!) What do you get

when you throw a million

books into the ocean? (A

title wave!) What is snake's

favorite subject? (Hiss-tory!)

Why did the teacher write on

the window? (To make the

lesson very clear!)

EASTER CROSSWORD

Easter, also known as Resurrection Day, is an annual spring holiday. It is a Christian celebration of Jesus Christ's resurrection from the dead. It is considered the most important day of the year by Christians. Non-Christians may observe Easter as the start of the spring season. Even if they do not regularly attend church, many people attend an Easter service.

Every year, Easter is not celebrated on the same day. This is known as a moveable feast. Currently, all Christian churches agree on how to calculate the date. Easter is observed on the first Sunday following the first full moon after March 21st. This means it takes place in March or April. It could happen as early as March 22 or as late as April 25.

KIDS crossword

"Happy Easter day"

APRIL 12

D	A	X	Q	P	C	X	E	C	L
T	P	T	V	J	H	C	F	A	S
V	R	T	U	L	I	P	S	R	T
L	I	M	A	A	C	Z	U	R	V
Q	L	A	M	B	K	S	B	O	B
Y	C	H	O	C	O	L	A	T	E
L	Y	G	R	A	S	S	S	L	G
C	W	B	E	A	N	S	K	R	G
D	M	N	D	H	R	H	E	S	S
R	L	Q	Q	H	U	N	T	M	N

BASKET
CHICK
CHOCOLATE
HUNT
CARROT
LAMB
EGGS
BEANS
TULIPS
APRIL
GRASS

HEALTHY GREENS CROSSWORD

Humans have consumed leafy greens since prehistoric times. However, it wasn't until the first Africans arrived in North America in the early 1600s that the continent got its first real taste of dark green leafy vegetables, which the grew for themselves and their families. Cooked greens evolved into a traditional African American food over tim. They eventually became essential in Southern regional diets and are now enjoyed across the country.

Dark green leafy vegetables are high in nutrients. Salad greens, kale, and spinach are high in vitamins A, C, E, and K, while broccoli, bok choy, and mustard are high in various B vitamins. These vegetables are also high in carotenoids, which are antioxidants that protect cells and help to prevent cancer in its early stages. They are also high in fiber, iron, magnesium, potassium, and calcium. Greens also have a low carbohydrate, sodium, and cholesterol content.

KiDS crossword

"Healthy greens"

U	V	B	E	A	N	S	N	T	F	J
O	I	A	V	O	C	A	D	O	M	T
W	N	Z	U	C	C	H	I	N	I	F
Q	P	N	C	U	C	U	M	B	E	R
E	F	E	C	A	B	B	A	G	E	Z
C	A	U	L	I	F	L	O	W	E	R
P	E	V	S	Q	U	A	S	H	A	D
E	B	A	R	T	I	C	H	O	K	E
A	G	B	R	O	C	C	O	L	I	Y
S	P	R	O	U	T	S	F	P	N	B
U	Z	A	S	P	A	R	A	G	U	S

ARTICHOKE
SQUASH
BROCCOLI
CAULIFLOWER
CUCUMBER
CABBAGE
ASPARAGUS
AVOCADO
ZUCCHINI
BEANS
PEAS
SPROUTS

Brain Teaser: Spot the Difference

1. You have to remember what you see in one picture and compare it to what you see in the other picture
2. You have to mark or circle the locations where you see a difference

Ready! Set! Go!

FIND 7 DIFFERENCES

Brain Teaser: Spot the Difference

1. You have to remember what you see in one picture and compare it to what you see in the other picture
2. You have to mark or circle the locations where you see a difference

Ready! Set! Go!

FIND
6
DIFFERENCES

Brain Teaser: Spot the Difference

1. You have to remember what you see in one picture and compare it to what you see in the other picture
2. You have to mark or circle the locations where you see a difference

Ready! Set! Go!

FIND 7 DIFFERENCES

Brain Teaser: Spot the Difference

1. You have to remember what you see in one picture and compare it to what you see in the other picture
2. You have to mark or circle the locations where you see a difference

Ready! Set! Go!

4th Grade Life Skills: Peer Pressure

First, read the entire passage. After that, go back and fill in the blanks. You can skip the blanks you're unsure about and finish them later.

impact	drink	trust	struggling	influence
positive	negative	classmates	avoid	victim

Almost all of us will come into contact with the apparent problem of peer pressure or the feeling that we have to do something because our friends or _____ think it is cool. Peer pressure can be a serious issue, whether we're talking about fourth-graders being pressured to play games, they don't want to play, or college students being pressured to smoke or _____ alcohol. As you get older, you'll realize you're responsible for the peer pressure you're subjected to and inadvertently exert on others. Though you can never completely eliminate peer pressure, you can mitigate some of its negative effects.

Peers have an _____ on your life, even if you are unaware of it, simply by spending time with you. You learn from them, and they do the same for you. It's only natural to listen to and learn from people your own age.

Peers can have a _____ impact on one another. Perhaps another student in your science class taught you an easy way to remember the planets in the solar system, or someone on your soccer team taught you a cool ball trick. You might look up to a friend who is always a good sport and try to emulate him or her. Perhaps you piqued the interest of others in your new favorite book, and now everyone is reading it. These are examples of how peers positively _____ one another daily.

Peers can have a _____ influence on one another. For example, a few kids at school may try to persuade you to skip class with them, a soccer friend may try to convince you to be mean to another player and never pass the ball to her, or a kid in the neighborhood may try to persuade you to shoplift with him.

It is common for kids to fall _____ to the pressure of their peers because they want to be liked, to fit in, or because they are afraid that other kids will make fun of them if they don't follow suit. Others join in because they want to try something new that others are doing. The notion that "everyone is doing it" can lead some children to disregard their better judgment or common sense.

You've probably heard your parents or teachers tell you to "pick your friends wisely." Peer pressure is a major reason for this. If you choose friends who don't do drugs, skip class, smoke cigarettes, or lie to their parents, you're less likely to do the same, even if other kids do. Try to assist a friend who is _____ to resist peer pressure. It can be powerful for one child to simply say, "I'm with you - let's go."

Even if you're alone and subjected to peer pressure, there are things you can do. You can _____ peers who put you under pressure to do things you know are wrong. You can say "no" and walk away. Even better, find other friends and classmates to hang out with.

If you continue to experience peer pressure and find it challenging to deal with, talk to someone you _____. If you've made a mistake or two, don't feel bad about it. Talking to a parent, teacher, or school counselor can make you feel much better and prepare you for peer pressure the next time you are subjected to it.

4th Grade Grammar: Nouns, Verbs, Adjectives

DIRECTIONS: SORT the words (below) by their corresponding *part-of-speech*.

color	chickens	kittens	banjo	library	goldfish
grieving	adorable	cough	stand	nasty	powerful
dance	build	cry	break	easy	circle
coach	aggressive	careful	eat	adventurous	think
mysterious	face	sticks	drink	guitar	busy
calm	window	worm	coast	draw	polka dot
eager	handsome	explain			

Nouns (13)	Verbs (13)	Adjectives (13)
coast	break	adorable
polka dot	build	busy
sticks	coach	eager
banjo	color	grieving
goldfish	cough	easy
chickens	think	calm
window	cry	handsome
face	dance	careful
library	draw	adventurous
circle	drink	aggressive
guitar	eat	mysterious
kittens	explain	nasty
worm	stand	powerful

*Usage Activity: CHOOSE (12) words from your completed table & WRITE (1) sentence for each form of the words you chose.

[Student worksheet has a 25 line writing exercise here.]

4th Grade Grammar: Compound Nouns

A compound noun is one that is composed of two or more words. Each word contributes to the meaning of the noun.

Compound nouns can be written three ways:

A single word	Two words	Hyphenated
haircut	rain forest	self-esteem

Instructions: Match the compound noun pairs correctly.

O	Fund	→	raiser
D	News	→	paper
C	Sun	→	glasses
F	Child	→	hood
N	Door	→	way
E	heart	→	attack
J	tooth	→	paste
K	apple	→	sauce
M	full	→	moon
H, B	hair	→	cut
G	air	→	plane
I	ear	→	ring
A	scare	→	crow
P	post	→	office
B, H	hair	→	dresser
L	note	→	book

4th Grade Grammar: Collective Noun

A collective noun is a noun that refers to a group of people, animals, or things. They are described as a single entity. Collective nouns are distinct from singular nouns in that singular nouns describe only one person or object.

Many collective nouns are common nouns, but when they are the name of a company or other organization with more than one person, such as Microsoft, they can also be proper nouns.

Find the collective noun in each sentence.

1. Our class visited the natural history museum on a field trip.

   class

2. The bison herd stampeded across the prairie, leaving a massive dust cloud in its wake.

   herd

3. We eagerly awaited the verdict of the jury.

   jury

4. This year's basketball team features three players who stand taller than six feet.

   team

5. At Waterloo, Napoleon's army was finally defeated.

   army

6. The plans for a new park have been approved by the town council.

   council

7. He comes from a large family, as the oldest of eleven children.

   family

8. The rock group has been on tour for several months.

   group

9. When Elvis appeared on stage, the entire audience erupted in applause.

   audience

10. The San Francisco crowd were their usual individualistic selves.

    crowd

11. The crew of sailors boarded the ships.

    crew

12. A mob destroyed the company's new office.

    mob

13. The fleet of ships was waiting at the port.

    fleet

14. It was difficult for the committee to come to a decision.

    committee

4th Grade Grammar: Concrete & Abstract Noun

the English language, both concrete and abstract nouns are essential parts of speech. The primary distinction between concrete and abstract nouns is that concrete nouns refer to people, places, or things that take up physical space, whereas abstract nouns refer to intangible ideas that annot be physically interacted with.

Vords like "luck," "disgust," and "empathy" are examples of abstract nouns. While it is possible to see someone being empathetic, empathy is not visible or tangible entity. The majority of feelings, emotions, and philosophies can be classified as abstract nouns.

1. FIND THE ABSTRACT NOUN ?

    a. KIND

    b. BOOK

2. FIND THE CONCRETE NOUNS

    a. WINDOW

    b. LOVE

3. FIND THE ABTRACT NOUN: THE KING WAS KNOWN FOR HIS JUSTICE

    a. JUSTICE

    b. KING

4. WHAT ARE THE 5 CONCRETE NOUNS

    a. TASTE, SMELL. WALKING, EYEING. TOUCHING

    b. SMELL,TASTE, SIGHT, HEARING,TOUCH

5. WHICH NOUN BELOW IS AN ABSTRACT NOUN?

    a. TRAIN

    b. LOVE

6. IS THE FOLLOWING NOUN CONCRETE OR ABSTRACT? CUPCAKES

    a. ABSTRACT

    b. CONCRETE

7. WHAT IS A CONCRETE NOUN?

    a. A NOUN THAT YOU CAN EXPERIENCE WITH AT LEAST 1 OF YOUR 5 SENSES.

    b. A NOUN THAT YOU CAN'T EXPERIENCE WITH AT LEAST 1 OF YOUR 5 SENSES.

8. WHICH WORD BELOW IS AN ABSTRACT NOUN?

    a. BRAVERY

    b. FRIEND

9. WHICH WORD BELOW IS NOT A CONCRETE NOUN?

    a. HAMBURGER

    b. ANGER

10. IS THE WORD THOUGHTFULNESS A CONCRETE OR ABSTRACT NOUN?

    a. ABSTRACT

    b. CONCRETE

ANSWERS

Reading Bar Graphs

Answer the following questions based off the bar graph.

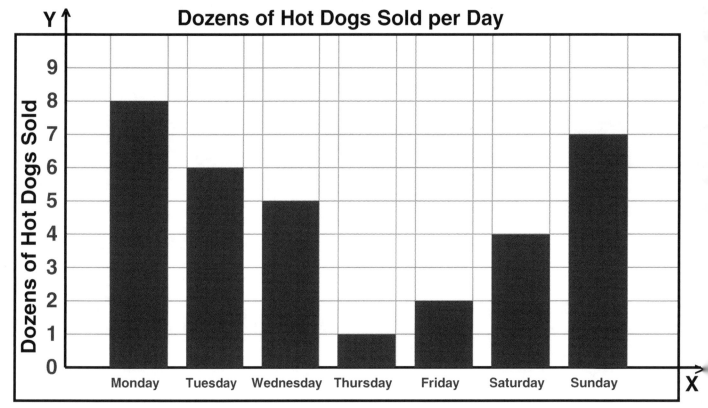

How many hot dogs were sold on Saturday and Tuesday combined?   120

How many more hot dogs were sold on Monday than on Thursday?   84

How many hot dogs were sold on Thursday, Friday, and Sunday?   120

Next week, we hope to sell twice as many hot dogs as we did this week. How many hot dogs will that be?   792

Were more hot dogs sold on Monday or on Thursday?   Monday

ANSWERS

Round each number to the nearest tens.

1) $\quad$ 712 $\longrightarrow$ 710
   $\quad$ - 397 $\longrightarrow$ - 400
   $\quad\quad$ 315 $\quad\quad\quad\quad$ 310

2) $\quad$ 428 $\longrightarrow$ 430
   $\quad$ - 232 $\longrightarrow$ - 230
   $\quad\quad$ 196 $\quad\quad\quad\quad$ 200

3) $\quad$ 716 $\longrightarrow$ 720
   $\quad$ + 479 $\longrightarrow$ + 480
   $\quad\quad$ 1195 $\quad\quad\quad\quad$ 1200

4) $\quad$ 514 $\longrightarrow$ 510
   $\quad$ + 133 $\longrightarrow$ + 130
   $\quad\quad$ 647 $\quad\quad\quad\quad$ 640

5) $\quad$ 935 $\longrightarrow$ 940
   $\quad$ - 188 $\longrightarrow$ - 190
   $\quad\quad$ 747 $\quad\quad\quad\quad$ 750

6) $\quad$ 481 $\longrightarrow$ 480
   $\quad$ + 131 $\longrightarrow$ + 130
   $\quad\quad$ 612 $\quad\quad\quad\quad$ 610

7) $\quad$ 798 $\longrightarrow$ 800
   $\quad$ - 647 $\longrightarrow$ - 650
   $\quad\quad$ 151 $\quad\quad\quad\quad$ 150

8) $\quad$ 484 $\longrightarrow$ 480
   $\quad$ + 235 $\longrightarrow$ + 240
   $\quad\quad$ 719 $\quad\quad\quad\quad$ 720

9) $\quad$ 939 $\longrightarrow$ 940
   $\quad$ + 548 $\longrightarrow$ + 550
   $\quad\quad$ 1487 $\quad\quad\quad\quad$ 1490

10) $\quad$ 692 $\longrightarrow$ 690
    $\quad$ + 542 $\longrightarrow$ + 540
    $\quad\quad$ 1234 $\quad\quad\quad\quad$ 1230

11) $\quad$ 414 $\longrightarrow$ 410
    $\quad$ + 921 $\longrightarrow$ + 920
    $\quad\quad$ 1335 $\quad\quad\quad\quad$ 1330

12) $\quad$ 224 $\longrightarrow$ 220
    $\quad$ - 154 $\longrightarrow$ - 150
    $\quad\quad$ 70 $\quad\quad\quad\quad$ 70

13) $\quad$ 321 $\longrightarrow$ 320
    $\quad$ - 257 $\longrightarrow$ - 260
    $\quad\quad$ 64 $\quad\quad\quad\quad$ 60

14) $\quad$ 295 $\longrightarrow$ 300
    $\quad$ - 182 $\longrightarrow$ - 180
    $\quad\quad$ 113 $\quad\quad\quad\quad$ 120

Time Answer Sheet

What time is on the clock? _____ 6:00

What time will it be in 4 hours and 20 minutes? _____ 10:20

What time was it 1 hour and 40 minutes ago? _____ 4:20

What time will it be in 3 hours ? _____ 9:00

What time is on the clock? _____ 12:40

What time will it be in 1 hour and 40 minutes? _____ 2:20

What time was it 2 hours and 20 minutes ago? _____ 10:20

What time will it be in 1 hour ? _____ 1:40

What time is on the clock? _____ 2:40

What time will it be in 3 hours and 40 minutes? _____ 6:20

What time was it 1 hour and 20 minutes ago? _____ 1:20

What time will it be in 4 hours ? _____ 6:40

What time is on the clock? _____ 6:20

What time will it be in 4 hours ? _____ 10:20

What time was it 2 hours and 20 minutes ago? _____ 3:60

What time will it be in 2 hours ? _____ 8:20

ANSWERS

Write the Numbers in Standard Form.

1) __884__ 800 + 80 + 4

2) __448__ 400 + 40 + 8

3) __530__ 500 + 30 + 0

4) __977__ 900 + 70 + 7

5) __312__ 300 + 10 + 2

6) __618__ 600 + 10 + 8

7) __868__ 800 + 60 + 8

8) __890__ 800 + 90 + 0

9) __556__ 500 + 50 + 6

10) __377__ 300 + 70 + 7

11) __567__ 500 + 60 + 7

12) __948__ 900 + 40 + 8

13) __787__ 700 + 80 + 7

14) __710__ 700 + 10 + 0

15) __984__ 900 + 80 + 4

answers

How Much Time Has Elapsed ?

1)   1:40 P.M.   to   7:35 P.M.   5 Hours & 55 Minutes

2)   1:20 A.M.   to   6:49 A.M.   5 Hours & 29 Minutes

3)   6:40 P.M.   to   8:24 P.M.   1 Hours & 44 Minutes

4)   2:40 P.M.   to   12:31 A.M.   9 Hours & 51 Minutes

5)   2:20 A.M.   to   5:46 A.M.   3 Hours & 26 Minutes

6)   2:00 A.M.   to   10:14 A.M.   8 Hours & 14 Minutes

7)   10:00 A.M. to   12:57 P.M.   2 Hours & 57 Minutes

8)   6:40 A.M.   to   10:17 A.M.   3 Hours & 37 Minutes

9)   9:40 P.M.   to   1:52 A.M.   4 Hours & 12 Minutes

10) 6:20 P.M.   to   11:57 P.M.   5 Hours & 37 Minutes

11) 2:00 A.M.   to   3:45 A.M.   1 Hours & 45 Minutes

12) 8:00 A.M.   to   2:54 P.M.   6 Hours & 54 Minutes

13) 12:40 A.M. to   2:50 A.M.   2 Hours & 10 Minutes

14) 11:20 P.M. to   8:39 A.M.   9 Hours & 19 Minutes

15) 9:00 P.M.   to   1:58 A.M.   4 Hours & 58 Minutes

Answers
Drawing Bar Graphs

raph the given information as a bar graph.

Day	# of Hot Dogs Sold
Monday	96
Tuesday	24
Wednesday	48
Thursday	72
Friday	60
Saturday	36
Sunday	12

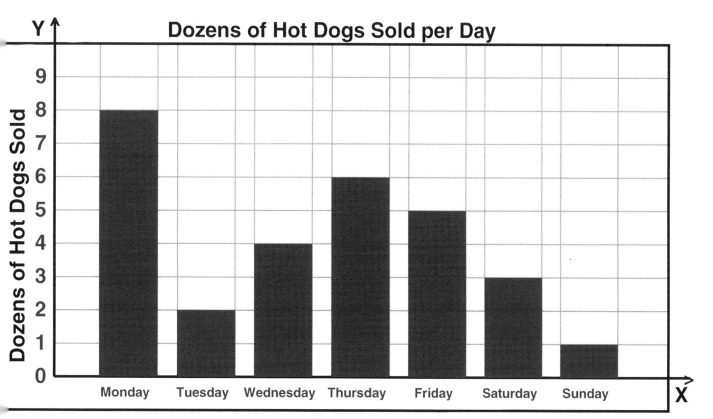

ANSWERS

Complete the Skip Counting Series

1)   19,   17,   15,   13,   11,   9,   7,   5,   3,   1

2)   74,   55,   36,   17,   -2,   -21,   -40,   -59,   -78,   -97

3)   59,   50,   41,   32,   23,   14,   5,   -4,   -13,   -22

4)   75,   80,   85,   90,   95,   100,   105,   110,   115,   120

5)   88,   98,   108,   118,   128,   138,   148,   158,   168,   178

6)   77,   86,   95,   104,   113,   122,   131,   140,   149,   158

7)   86,   75,   64,   53,   42,   31,   20,   9,   -2,   -13

8)   90,   75,   60,   45,   30,   15,   0,   -15,   -30,   -45

9)   33,   28,   23,   18,   13,   8,   3,   -2,   -7,   -12

10)   19,   27,   35,   43,   51,   59,   67,   75,   83,   91

11)   20,   24,   28,   32,   36,   40,   44,   48,   52,   56

12)   30,   27,   24,   21,   18,   15,   12,   9,   6,   3

ANSWERS

Addition Worksheet

53125	893724	7754653	40034
58540	759775	8766279	70732
79810	403688	7714657	43161
+ 11737	+ 200969	+ 4524724	+ 41196
203212	2258156	28760313	195123

192189	2241377	84097	413796
965026	7928905	19687	877734
531938	5984195	69704	997766
+ 385320	+ 8264879	+ 21157	+ 742703
2074473	24419356	194645	3031999

7059169	86799	636053	6947438
5369228	28259	120921	8770263
9985601	90783	897238	9488267
+ 8707044	+ 14295	+ 447023	+ 9910513
31121042	220136	2101235	35116481

35283	189936	7019570	24476
17919	753760	1010287	75122
61158	617906	5621292	61687
+ 49632	+ 863520	+ 5479675	+ 55646
163992	2425122	19130824	216931

ANSWERS

MISSING NUMBERS

1) $N \times 23 = 759$ N = <u>33</u>   2) $N - 23 = 16$ N = <u>39</u>

3) $N \div 40 = 14$ N = <u>560</u>   4) $N - 14 = 1$ N = <u>15</u>

5) $34 + N = 55$ N = <u>21</u>   6) $N - 17 = 13$ N = <u>30</u>

7) $25 - N = 4$ N = <u>21</u>   8) $N \times 22 = 770$ N = <u>35</u>

9) $17 + N = 49$ N = <u>32</u>   10) $N - 37 = 3$ N = <u>40</u>

11) $N \div 31 = 12$ N = <u>372</u>   12) $32 + N = 69$ N = <u>37</u>

13) $37 - N = 12$ N = <u>25</u>   14) $14 \times N = 420$ N = <u>30</u>

15) $N + 30 = 56$ N = <u>26</u>   16) $N + 30 = 61$ N = <u>31</u>

17) $24 - N = 2$ N = <u>22</u>   18) $31 \times N = 775$ N = <u>25</u>

19) $30 + N = 60$ N = <u>30</u>   20) $N \times 13 = 156$ N = <u>12</u>

21) $N \div 21 = 38$ N = <u>798</u>   22) $N \div 29 = 40$ N = <u>1160</u>

23) $40 \times N = 600$ N = <u>15</u>   24) $N \times 10 = 310$ N = <u>31</u>

25) $28 + N = 68$ N = <u>40</u>   26) $361 \div N = 19$ N = <u>19</u>

27) $253 \div N = 11$ N = <u>23</u>   28) $27 + N = 51$ N = <u>24</u>

29) $N \times 11 = 209$ N = <u>19</u>   30) $N \div 32 = 36$ N = <u>1152</u>

Division

$110 \div 10 = 11$	$35 \div 7 = 5$	$90 \div 9 = 10$
$3 \div 1 = 3$	$66 \div 11 = 6$	$9 \div 9 = 1$
$8 \div 4 = 2$	$60 \div 5 = 12$	$48 \div 8 = 6$
$45 \div 5 = 9$	$9 \div 3 = 3$	$90 \div 9 = 10$
$24 \div 12 = 2$	$24 \div 6 = 4$	$35 \div 5 = 7$
$48 \div 4 = 12$	$28 \div 4 = 7$	$12 \div 12 = 1$
$8 \div 1 = 8$	$60 \div 6 = 10$	$50 \div 10 = 5$
$4 \div 2 = 2$	$14 \div 2 = 7$	$132 \div 11 = 12$
$42 \div 7 = 6$	$22 \div 2 = 11$	$54 \div 6 = 9$
$80 \div 10 = 8$	$9 \div 3 = 3$	$40 \div 8 = 5$

ANSWERS

What is the Fraction of the Shaded Area ?

1) $\dfrac{3}{4}$

6) $\dfrac{3}{5}$

2) $\dfrac{1}{3}$

7) $\dfrac{7}{8}$

3) $\dfrac{3}{5}$

8) $\dfrac{2}{3}$

4) $\dfrac{6}{8}$

9) $\dfrac{3}{8}$

5) $\dfrac{2}{5}$

10) $\dfrac{2}{5}$

Shade the Figure with the Indicated Fraction.

11) $\dfrac{1}{2}$

16) $\dfrac{4}{8}$

12) $\dfrac{1}{4}$

17) $\dfrac{4}{5}$

13) $\dfrac{1}{5}$

18) $\dfrac{1}{8}$

14) $\dfrac{5}{8}$

19) $\dfrac{2}{4}$

15) $\dfrac{2}{8}$

20) $\dfrac{4}{5}$

4th Grade Science: Vertebrates

o begin, all animals are classified as either vertebrates or invertebrates. Invertebrates lack a backbone, whereas vertebrates do. Scientists can't op there, because each group contains thousands of different animals! As a result, scientists divide vertebrates and invertebrates into creasingly smaller groups. Let's talk about vertebrates and some of their classifications.

ertebrates range in size from a frog to a blue whale. Because there are at least 59,000 different types of vertebrates on the planet, they are rther classified into five major groups: mammals, birds, fish, amphibians, and reptiles. Remember that animals are classified into these groups ased on what they have in common. Why is an elephant classified as a mammal while a crocodile is classified as a reptile? Let's go over some of e characteristics of each vertebrate group.

arm-blooded animals are mammals. This means that their bodies maintain their temperature, which is usually higher than the temperature of the rrounding air. They also have hair or fur; they have lungs to breathe air; that they feed milk to their babies; and that most give birth to live young, ther than laying eggs, as a dog does.

- Birds have feathers, two wings (though not all birds, such as the ostrich and penguin, can fly), are warm-blooded, and lay eggs.
- Fish have fins or scales, live in water, and breathe oxygen through gills.
- Like salamanders and frogs, Amphibians have smooth, moist skin (amphibians must keep their skin wet); lay eggs in water; most breathe through their skin and lungs.
- Reptiles have scales (imagine a scaly lizard), are cold-blooded (their body temperature changes as the temperature around them changes), breathe air. Most reptiles, including the crocodile and snake, lay hard-shelled eggs on land.

ertebrates play several vital roles in an ecosystem. Many predator species are large vertebrates in ecosystems. Lions, eagles, and sharks are amples of predatory vertebrates. Many prey species in ecosystems are also vertebrates. Mice, rabbits, and frogs are examples of these imals. Many vertebrates serve as scavengers in ecosystems. They are significant because they remove dead animals from the environment. rkey vultures and hyenas, for example, are both vertebrate scavengers. Furthermore, many vertebrates serve as pollinators in ecosystems. ts and monkeys, for example, may aid in pollen spread by visiting various trees and plants.

umans value vertebrates for a variety of reasons. Vertebrates are domesticated animals used by humans. These animals are capable of oducing milk, food, and clothing. They can also help with work. Agricultural animals are usually vertebrates. Humans also hunt a variety of wild rtebrate animals for food.

1. Vertebrates range in _____ from a frog to a blue whale.
   - a. age
   - b. size

2. Fish have fins or scales, live in water, and breathe ___ through gills.
   - a. oxygen
   - b. water

3. Invertebrates lack a _____, whereas vertebrates _____.
   - a. skin, whereas vertebrates do
   - b. backbone, whereas vertebrates do

4. Warm-blooded animals are _____.
   - a. mammals
   - b. producers

5. Some vertebrates serve as _____, they remove dead animals from the environment.
   - a. scavengers
   - b. invertebrates

6. Lions, eagles, and sharks are examples of _____ vertebrates.
   - a. ecofriendly
   - b. predatory

7. _____ animals are capable of producing milk, food, and clothing.
   - a. Non-producing
   - b. Domesticated

8. Many vertebrates serve as _____ in ecosystems, they may aid in pollen spread by visiting various trees and plants.
   - a. water lilies
   - b. pollinators

4th Grade Science:
Invertebrates

Invertebrates can be found almost anywhere. Invertebrates account for at least 95% of all animals on the planet! Do you know what one thing they all have in common? Invertebrates lack a backbone.

Your body is supported by a backbone, which protects your organs and connects your other bones. As a result, you are a vertebrate. On the other hand, invertebrates lack the support of bones, so their bodies are often simpler, softer, and smaller. They are also cold-blooded, which means their body temperature fluctuates in response to changes in the air or water around them.

Invertebrates can be found flying, swimming, crawling, or floating and provide essential services to the environment and humans. Nobody knows how many different types of invertebrates there are, but there are millions!

Just because an invertebrate lacks a spinal column does not mean it does not need to eat. Invertebrates, like all other forms of animal life, must obtain nutrients from their surroundings. Invertebrates have evolved two types of digestion to accomplish this. The use of intracellular digestion is common in the most simple organisms. The food is absorbed into the cell and broken down in the cytoplasm at this point. Extracellular digestion, in which cells break down food through the secretion of enzymes and other techniques, is used by more advanced invertebrates. All vertebrates use extracellular digestion.

Still, all animals, invertebrates or not, need a way to get rid of waste. Most invertebrates, especially the simplest ones, use the process of diffusion to eliminate waste. This is merely the opposite of intracellular digestion. However, more advanced invertebrates have more advanced waste disposal mechanisms. Similar to our kidneys, specialized glands in these animals filter and excrete waste. But there is a happy medium. Even though some invertebrates do not have complete digestive tracts like vertebrates, they do not simply flush out waste through diffusion. Instead, the mouth doubles as an exit.

Scientists have classified invertebrates into numerous groups based on what the animals have in common. Arthropods have segmented bodies, which means that they are divided into sections. Consider an ant!

Arthropods are the most numerous group of invertebrates. They can live on land, as spiders and insects do, or in water, as crayfish and crabs do. Because insects are the most numerous group of arthropods, many of them fly, including mosquitoes, bees, locusts, and ladybugs.

They also have jointed legs or limbs to help them walk, similar to how you have knees for your legs and elbows for your arms. The majority of arthropods have an exoskeleton, tough outer skin, or shell that protects their body. Have you ever wondered why when you squish a bug, it makes that crunching sound? That's right; it's the exoskeleton!

Mollusks are the second most numerous group of invertebrates. They have soft bodies and can be found on land or in water. Shells protect the soft bodies of many mollusks, including snails, oysters, clams, and scallops. However, not all, such as octopus, squid, and cuttlefish, have a shell.

1. Invertebrates lack a _____.
   a. backbone
   b. tailbone

2. Invertebrates are also _____.
   a. cold-blooded
   b. warm-blooded

3. _____ can live on land, as spiders and insects do, or in water, as crayfish and crabs do.
   a. Vertebrates
   b. Arthropods

4. All animals, invertebrates or not, need a way to get rid of _____.
   a. their skin
   b. waste

5. _____ have soft bodies and can be found on land or in water.
   a. Arthropods
   b. Mollusks

6. Just because an invertebrate lacks a _____ column does not mean it does not need to eat.
   a. spinal
   b. tissues

7. Your body is supported by a backbone, which protects your _____ and connects your other bones.
   a. organs
   b. muscles

8. Invertebrates lack the support of bones, so their bodies are often simpler, ___, and smaller.
   a. softer and bigger
   b. softer and smaller

4th Grade Science: Organelles

Do you and your dog have a similar appearance? We are all aware that people and dogs appear to be very different on the outside. However, there are some similarities on the inside. Cells make up all animals, including humans and dogs.

All animal cells appear to be the same. They have a cell membrane that contains cytoplasm, which is a gooey fluid. Organelles float in the cytoplasm. Organelles function as tiny machines that meet the needs of the cell. The term organelle refers to a "miniature organ." This lesson will teach you about the various organelles found in animal cells and what they do.

The nucleus of the cell is the cell's brain. It is in charge of many of the cell's functions. The nucleus is where DNA, the genetic instructions for building your body, is stored. DNA contains vital information! Your nucleus has its membrane to protect this essential information, similar to the membrane that surrounds the entire cell.

Your cells require energy. Energy is produced by mitochondria, which are oval-shaped organelles. Mitochondria convert the nutrients that enter the cell into ATP. Your cells use ATP for energy. Because they are the cell's powerhouses, you might think of these organelles as the mighty mitochondria.

The nutrients must be digested before they can be converted into energy by the mitochondria. Digestion is carried out by a group of organelles known as lysosomes. Digestive enzymes are found in lysosomes. Enzymes can sometimes be released into the cell. Because the enzymes kill the cell, lysosomes are known as "suicide bags."

Use Google or your preferred source to help match each term with a definition.

L	nucleus	⇢	where DNA is stored
B	lysosomes	⇢	degradation of proteins and cellular waste
J	Golgi Apparatus	⇢	modification of proteins; "post-office" of the cell
I	Mitochondria	⇢	powerhouse of the cell
D	SER	⇢	lipid synthesis
K	RER	⇢	protein synthesis + modifications
A	Microtubules	⇢	responsible for chromosome segregation
C	ribosomes	⇢	protein synthesis
H	peroxysomes	⇢	degradation of H2O2
G	cell wall	⇢	prevents excessive uptake of water, protects the cell (in plants)
E	chloroplast	⇢	site of photosynthesis
F	central vacuole	⇢	stores water in plant cells

WATER CYCLE ANSWERS

1. NMSALIITBOU   s u b l i m a t i o n

2. IARTASRPONTIN   t r a n s p i r a t i o n

3. OMLLECUE   m o l e c u l e

4. NEIRAVOTAOP   e v a p o r a t i o n

5. ALEIGCR   g l a c i e r

6. TONOINSNCEDA   c o n d e n s a t i o n

7. DARRWOGENTU   g r o u n d w a t e r

8. TUNLOPLAT   p o l l u t a n t

9. EPITITARINCPO   p r e c i p i t a t i o n

10. ITNIOILRNFAT   i n f i l t r a t i o n

11. ODRLPET   d r o p l e t

12. NIEDTSOPIO   d e p o s i t i o n

13. WTAEERH   w e a t h e r

14. EONNTIGR   n i t r o g e n

15. RWANTREAI   r a i n w a t e r

16. REBGICE   i c e b e r g

17. TNOAIADRI   r a d i a t i o n

18. EOXNGY   o x y g e n

19. SGOMRNIA   o r g a n i s m

20. YNEDRHOG   h y d r o g e n

21. EARTLWTME   m e l t w a t e r

22. COTNCLEOLI   c o l l e c t i o n

23. PAROV   v a p o r

24. NEVOEMTM   m o v e m e n t

25. ORENINTNVEM   e n v i r o n m e n t

26. OCSANE   o c e a n s

4th Grade Science: The Seasons

ur __planet__ has four seasons each year: autumn, winter, spring, and __summer__ .

he Earth spins in a slightly tilted position as it orbits the sun (on an axis tilted 23.5 degrees from a straight-up, vertical position). Because different parts of e planet are angled towards or away from the sun's light throughout the year, this tilt causes our seasons. More or less sunlight and heat influence the ngth of each day, the average daily temperature, and the amount of rainfall in different seasons.

he tilt has two major effects: the sun's angle to the Earth and the length of the days. The Earth is tilted so that the __North__ Pole is more pointed towards e sun for half of the year. The South Pole is pointing at the sun for the other half. When the North Pole is angled toward the sun, the days in the northern emisphere (north of the equator) receive more sunlight, resulting in longer days and shorter nights. The northern hemisphere __heats__ up and experiences ummer as the days lengthen. As the year progresses, the Earth's tilt shifts to the North Pole points away from the sun, resulting in winter.

s a result, seasons north of the equator are opposed to seasons south of the equator. When Europe and the United States are experiencing winter, Brazil ad Australia will be experiencing summer.

e discussed how the length of the day changes, but the angle of the sun also changes. In the summer, the sun __shines__ more directly on the Earth, oviding more energy to the surface and heating it. In the winter, sunlight strikes the Earth at an angle. This produces less energy and heats the Earthless.

e longest day in the Northern Hemisphere is __June__ 21st, while the longest night is December 21st. The opposite is true in the Southern Hemisphere, here December 21st is the longest day, and June 21st is the longest night. There are only two days a year when the day and night are the same. These are eptember 22nd and March 21st.

e amount of time it is light for decreases in autumn, and the __leaves__ begin to change color and fall off the trees. In the United States of America, autumn referred to as Fall.

nter brings colder weather, sometimes snow and __frost__ , no leaves on the trees, and the amount of daylight during the day are at its shortest.

e weather usually warms up in the spring, trees begin to sprout leaves, plants begin to bloom, and young animals such as __chicks__ and lambs are born.

e weather is usually warm in the summer, the trees have entire __green__ leaves, and the amount of daylight during the day is extended.

4th Grade History: United States Armed Forces

1. The United States military is divided into ___ branches.
   - a. six
   - b. five

2. _____ is managed by the United States Department of Homeland Security.
   - a. The National Guard
   - b. The Coast Guard

3. The _____ of the United States is the Commander in Chief of the United States Armed Forces.
   - a. Governor
   - b. President

4. The United States maintains a military to safeguard its _____ and interests.
   - a. borders
   - b. cities

5. DoD is in charge of controlling each _____ of the military.
   - a. branch
   - b. army

6. The Marines are prepared to fight on both land and ____.
   - a. battlefield
   - b. sea

7. The United States Space Force is in charge of operating and defending military ____ and ground stations.
   - a. soldiers
   - b. satellites

8. The mission of the _____ is to defend the country from outside forces.
   - a. United States DoD Forces
   - b. United States Air Force

9. There are _____ units in all 50 states.
   - a. Army National Guard
   - b. Armed Nations Guard

10. The United States Navy conducts its missions at sea to secure and protect the world's _____.
    - a. oceans
    - b. borders

11. The primary concern of the United States Coast Guard is to protect_____.
    - a. domestic waterways
    - b. domesticated cities

12. The United States military is: the Amy Force, Army, Coast Guard, Mario Corps, Old Navy, and Space Force.
    - a. True
    - b. False

Extra Credit: Has America ever been invaded? (Independent student research answer)

[Student worksheet has a 19 line writing exercise here.]

4th Grade Government History:
How Laws Are Made

1. If the Senate approves the bill, it will be sent to the _____.
   a. President
   b. House Representee

2. The _____ may decide to make changes to the bill before it is passed.
   a. governor
   b. committee

3. The bill must then be _____ by a member of Congress.
   a. signed
   b. sponsored

4. The President has the option of refusing to sign the bill. This is known as a ___.
   a. voted
   b. veto

5. The Senate and House can choose to override the President's veto by _____ again.
   a. creating a new bill
   b. voting

6. The bill is assigned to a committee after it is _____.
   a. introduced
   b. vetoed

7. Bills are created and passed by _____.
   a. The House
   b. Congress

8. A bill must be signed into law by the President within ___-days.
   a. 10
   b. 5

9. The President's _____ is the final step in a bill becoming law.
   a. signature
   b. saying yes

10. If the committee agrees to pass the bill, it will be sent to the House or Senate's main ___ for approval.
    a. chamber
    b. state

tra Credit: What are some of the weirdest laws in the world? List at least 5. (Independent student's answers)

[Student worksheet has a 19 line writing exercise here.]

4th Grade History: The Vikings

During the __Middle__ Ages, the Vikings lived in Northern Europe. They first settled in the Scandinavian lands that are now Denmark, Sweden, and Norway. During the Middle Ages, the Vikings played a significant role in Northern Europe, particularly during the Viking Age, which lasted from 800 CE to 1066 CE.

In Old Norse, the word Viking means "to raid." The Vikings would board their longships and __sail__ across the seas to raid villages on Europe's northern coast, including islands like Great Britain. In 787 CE, they first appeared in England to raid villages. When the Vikings __raided__, they were known to attack defenseless monasteries. This earned them a bad reputation as barbarians, but monasteries were wealthy and undefended Viking targets.

The Vikings eventually began to __settle__ in areas other than Scandinavia. They colonized parts of Great Britain, Germany, and Iceland in the ninth century. They spread into northeastern Europe, including Russia, in the 10th century. They also established Normandy, which means "Northmen," along the coast of northern France.

By the beginning of the 11th century, the Vikings had reached the pinnacle of their power. Leif Eriksson, son of Erik the Red, was one Vikings who made it to __North__ America. He established a brief settlement in modern-day Canada. This was thousands of years before Columbus.

The English and King Harold Godwinson __defeated__ the Vikings, led by King Harald Hardrada of Norway, in 1066. The defeat in this battle is sometimes interpreted as the end of the Viking Age. The Vikings stopped expanding their territory at this point, and raids became less frequent.

The arrival of Christianity was a major factor at the end of the Viking age. The Vikings became more and more a part of mainland Europe as Scandinavia was converted to __Christianity__ and became a part of Christian Europe. Sweden's, Denmark's, and Norway's identities and borders began to emerge as well.

The Vikings were perhaps best known for their ships. The Vikings built longships for exploration and raiding. Longships were long, narrow vessels built for speed. Oars primarily propelled them but later added a sail to help in windy conditions. Longships had a shallow draft, which allowed them to float in __shallow__ water and land on beaches.

The Vikings also built __cargo__ ships known as Knarr for trading. The Knarr was wider and deeper than the longship, allowing it to transport more cargo.

Five recovered Viking ships can be seen at the Viking Ship Museum in Roskilde, __Denmark__. It's also possible to see how the Vikings built their ships. The Vikings used a shipbuilding technique known as clinker building. They used long wood planks that overlapped along the edges.

Extra Credit: Do Vikings still exist? (Independent student's answer)

[Student worksheet has a 14 line writing exercise here.]

4th Grade Science: Coral Reefs

ne of the most important marine __biomes__ is the coral reef.

oral reefs are home to approximately __25%__ of all known marine species, despite being a relatively small biome.

oral reefs may appear to be made of __rocks__ at first glance, but they are actually __living__ organisms.

hen polyps die, they __harden__ and new polyps grow on top of them, causing the reef to expand.

ecause polyps must eat to __survive__, you can think of the coral reef as eating as well.

ney eat plankton and __algae__, which are small animals.

__Photosynthesis__ is how algae get their food from the sun.

form, coral reefs require warm, __shallow__ water.

outheast Asia and the region around __Australia__ are home to a sizable portion of the world's coral reefs.

ne __Great__ Barrier Reef is 2,600 miles long.

__Fringe__ reefs are reefs that grow close to the shore.

__Barrier__ reef - Barrier reefs grow away from the shoreline, sometimes for several miles.

n __atoll__ is a coral ring that surrounds a lagoon of water. It begins as a fringe reef surrounding a volcanic island.

ome atolls are large enough to support human __habitation__.

4th Grade Storytime Reading:
The Wolf & 7 Kids

The story goes that once upon a time, an old Goat had seven little Kids and adored them with all the affection a mother would have for her children.

She wanted to go into the forest and get some food one day. So she called up all seven children to her and said, "Dear Children, I must go into the forest." Keep an eye out for the Wolf. If he gets in, he'll eat you whole-skin, hair, and all. The wretch frequently disguise himself, but you'll recognize him right away by his rough voice and black feet."

"Dear Mother, we will take good care of ourselves," the children said. You may leave without wariness."

It wasn't long before someone knocked on the door and yelled, "Open the door, dear Children! Your mother has arrived, and she has brought something for each of you."

The little Kids, however, recognized the Wolf by his rough voice. "We will not open the door," they cried, "because you are not our mother." Your voice is rough, whereas hers is soft and pleasant. "You are Wolf!"

However, the Wolf had placed his black paws against the window, and when the children saw them, they cried out, "We will not open the door; our mother does not have black feet like you." "You are Wolf!"

The Wolf then dashed over to a baker and said, "I've hurt my feet; rub some dough over them for me."

After rubbing his feet, the baker ran to the miller and said, "Strew some white meal over my feet for me." "The Wolf wants to deceive someone," the miller reasoned, and he refused. "If you don't do it," the Wolf said, "I will devour you." The miller became terrified and whitened his paws for him. Yes, and so are men!

Now, for the third time, the wretch went to the house-door, knocked, and said, "Open the door for me, Children!" Your dear little mother has returned home, and she has brought something from the forest for each of you."

Then he inserted his paws through the window. When the kids saw they were white, they believed everything he said and opened th door. But who else but the Wolf should enter?

They were terrified and wished to remain hidden. One jumped under the table , another into the bed, a third into the stove, a fourth int the kitchen, a fifth into the cupboard, a sixth into the washing bowl, and a seventh into the clock case. But the Wolf found them all and swallowed them down his throat one after the other. The only one he didn't find was the youngest in the clock case.

When the Wolf had satisfied his hunger , he exited the building, sat down under a tree in the green meadow outside, and fell asleep.

Soon after, the old Goat returned from the forest. What a sight she saw over there! The front door was wide open. The table, chairs, and benches were thrown to the ground, the washing bowl was shattered, and the quilts and pillows were yanked from the bed.

She took the Kid out, and it informed her that the Wolf had arrived and devoured all the others. You can only imagine how she cried ove her poor children!

In her grief, she eventually went out, and the youngest Kid followed her. When they arrived at the meadow, the Wolf by the tree was snoring so loudly that the branches shook. She examined him from every angle and noticed that something was moving and struggling in his stomach. "Ah!" she exclaimed, "is it possible that my poor children, whom he has devoured for his supper, are still alive?"

The Kid then had to dash home to get scissors , a needle and thread, and the Goat to cut open the monster's stomach. She had barely made one cut when a little Kid thrust its head out, and when she had cut further, all six sprang out one after the other, all still aliv and unharmed, because the monster had swallowed them whole in his greed.

There was a lot of joy! They ran up to their mother and jumped like a tailor at his wedding. "Now go and look for some big stones," the mother said. We'll stuff them into the wicked beast's stomach while he's sleeping."

When the Wolf awoke from his slumber, he rose to his feet, and because the stones in his stomach were making him thirsty, he desired to go to a well to drink. When he started walking and moving around, the stones in his stomach knocked against each other and rattled . Then he cried out:

And as he approached the well, stooped over the water , and was about to drink, the heavy stones caused him to fall in. There was n way to save him, so he had to drown!

4th Grade Spelling Words

Use the word bank to unscramble the words below.

bubble	community	reject	husband	pineapple	hostile
compass	tomatoes	alarm	salute	perhaps	fugitive
friends	council	fountain	goose	ankle	tutor
difference	center	hammer	jewel	choir	fatal
children	subject				

1. RNIEFDS   f r i e n d s

2. UGITIFVE   f u g i t i v e

3. EPLIPPNAE   p i n e a p p l e

4. RSEPAPH   p e r h a p s

5. COIRH   c h o i r

6. AOTFNUIN   f o u n t a i n

7. EGOSO   g o o s e

8. ERAMMH   h a m m e r

9. LOCNUIC   c o u n c i l

10. LHOTEIS   h o s t i l e

11. AALTF   f a t a l

12. JLEWE   j e w e l

13. CTIMMUNOY   c o m m u n i t y

14. ASCMPOS   c o m p a s s

15. LASUTE   s a l u t e

16. ESTUCJB   s u b j e c t

17. CLEDHNRI   c h i l d r e n

18. RCEEJT   r e j e c t

19. CIDFEFREEN   d i f f e r e n c e

20. NLEAK   a n k l e

21. HANDSUB   h u s b a n d

22. EECRTN   c e n t e r

23. MOSOTAET   t o m a t o e s

24. OURTT   t u t o r

25. RALMA   a l a r m

26. LEBUBB   b u b b l e

4th Grade Grammar: Sentence Building

Practice *sentence* building. U*nscramble* the words to form a complete sentence.

1. Germs can build up a resistance to antibiotics.

   antibiotics.   up   Germs   to   a   resistance

2. There was a sharp curve in the road.

   in   curve   road.   There   was   sharp

3. Let's make a graph with this data.

   make   this   a   with   data.

4. I like to eat turkey and mashed potatoes.

   turkey   mashed   to   eat   and   I

5. My sister built a house out of clay.

   clay.   of   out   house   sister   My

6. The flight was very long and boring.

   boring.   The   was   long   and

7. I heard that man is very wealthy.

   wealthy.   that   man   is   I

8. I will have soup and crackers for lunch.

   soup   have   I   and   lunch.   crackers

9. There is a brook behind my home.

   my   brook   home.   a   is

10. I like to drink water.

    I   like   water.   drink

11. How long have you had this sickness?

    sickness?   you   had   have   long

12. He wrote many books about elephants.

    many   wrote   about   He

13. My body temperature is normal. _____

    temperature · is · My · body

14. I have a weak stomach sometimes. _____

    weak · a · I · stomach

15. Stay still while I fix your tie. _____

    Stay · still · fix · I · tie.

16. My head started to ache this morning. _____

    started · to · My · ache · head

17. My big brother works in an office. _____

    My · works · big · in · brother

18. The train cars kept lurching forward. _____

    train · The · kept · lurching

19. I can't possibly make a prediction. _____

    prediction. · a · I · make

20. I like my school picture this year. _____

    I · like · picture · this · year.

21. Will the pizza have everything on it? _____

    the · it? · Will · on · everything

22. My cat is very dear to me. _____

    My · is · cat · me. · very

23. I want a friend, not an enemy. _____

    want · not · enemy. · friend, · an

24. Can you guess my weight? _____

    my · you · Can · weight?

4th Grade Geography: Castles in Germany

1. _____ is now the seat of the local government and an art museum.
   a. Schwerin Castle
   b. Swaziland Castle

2. Hohenzollern Castle is situated on the _____ of Mount Hohenzollern.
   a. crest
   b. end

3. The architecture of German castles consists of a combination of towers and _____.
   a. beautiful curtains
   b. fortified walls

4. German castles evolved during the "_____ Ages".
   a. Century
   b. Medieval

5. This castle was built as a residence rather than a fortress.
   a. Eltz Castle
   b. Schwerin Castle

6. Castles are now iconic symbols of magnificence and _____ tales.
   a. real life
   b. mythical

7. _____ has inspired poets for centuries.
   a. Schloss Heidelberg
   b. Steven Spielberg

8. _____ Castle is located in the Bavarian Alps near the town of Füssen.
   a. Norwegian
   b. Neuschwanstein

4th Grade Geography Vocabulary Crossword

Complete the crossword by filling in a word that fits each clue. Fill in the correct answers, one letter per square, both across and down, from the given clues. There will be a gray space between multi-word answers.

Tip: Solve the easy clues first, and then go back and answer the more difficult ones.

Crossword grid (answers):

- 24 Across: WETLAND
- 16 Across: OASIS
- 17 Across: PLATEAU
- 10 Across: FOG
- 11 Across: FROST
- 1 Across: BASIN
- 23 Across: VORTEX
- 18 Across: STEPPE
- 9 Across: DEW
- 20 Across: TOPOLOGY
- 12 Across: GLACIER
- 21 Across: TRENCH

Down answers visible: DALE, HAIL, CLIFF, COUNTRY, HALL, VALE, CAVERN, BAVASRNG (ICEBERG), DESERT, SMOG, ZEPHYR, BAY, MIST, TOPOLOGY

Across

1. a bowl-shaped vessel used for holding food or liquids
9. water that has condensed on a cool surface overnight
10. droplets of water vapor suspended in the air near the ground
11. ice crystals forming a white deposit
12. a slowly moving mass of ice
16. a shelter serving as a place of safety or sanctuary
17. a relatively flat highland
18. an extensive plain without trees
20. topographic study of a given place
21. a long steep-sided depression in the ocean floor
23. A circular, spiral, or helical motion in a fluid
24. a low area where the land is saturated with water

Down

2. an indentation of a shoreline smaller than a gulf
3. a large cave or a large chamber in a cave
4. a steep rock face
5. the shore of a sea or ocean
6. the territory occupied by a nation
7. an open valley in a hilly area
8. arid land with little or no vegetation
13. precipitation of ice pellets
14. a large frozen mass floating at sea
15. a thin fog with condensation near the ground
18. air pollution by a mixture of smoke and fog
23. a valley
25. a slight wind

GLACIER   ZEPHYR   ICEBERG
DESERT   FROST   DALE   HAIL
SMOG   BASIN   VALE   BAY
OASIS   COUNTRY   COAST
TOPOLOGY   WETLAND   MIST
STEPPE   VORTEX   PLATEAU
FOG   DEW   CLIFF   TRENCH
CAVERN

4th Grade Geography: Canada

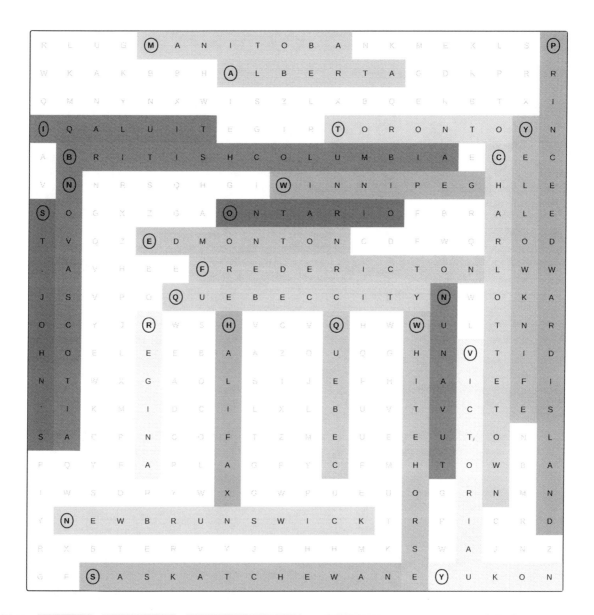

Yukon →   Nunavut ↓   Nova Scotia ↓   Prince Edward Island ↓   New Brunswick →   Quebec ↓   Ontario →   Manitoba →

Saskatchewan →   Alberta →   British Columbia →   Victoria ↓   Edmonton →   Regina ↓   Winnipeg →   Toronto →

Quebec City →   Fredericton →   Charlottetown ↓   Halifax ↓   St. John's ↓   Iqaluit →   Yellowknife ↓   Whitehorse ↓

24 words in Wordsearch: 11 vertical, 13 horizontal, 0 diagonal. (0 reversed.)

4th Grade Music: Instruments

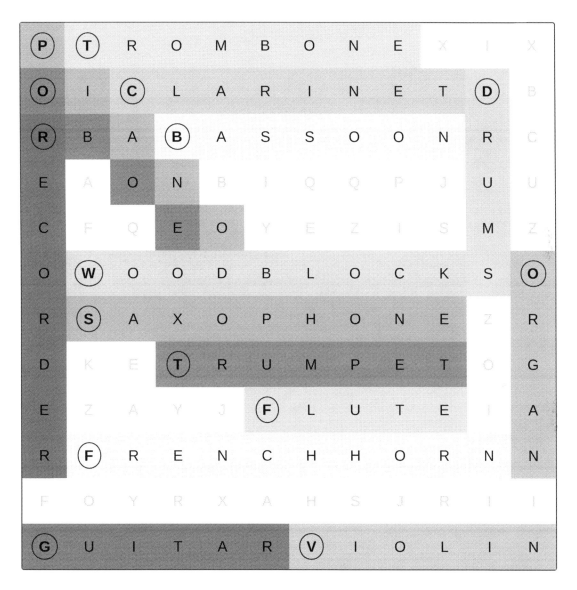

PIANO ↘   FLUTE →   BASSOON →   CLARINET →   TROMBONE →   VIOLIN →

WOODBLOCK →   TRUMPET →   OBOE ↘   SAXOPHONE →   GUITAR →   DRUMS ↓

ORGAN ↓   RECORDER ↓   FRENCH HORN →

15 words in Wordsearch: 3 vertical, 10 horizontal, 2 diagonal. (0 reversed.)

4th Grade Music: Musical Terms

Complete the crossword by filling in a word that fits each clue. Fill in the correct answers, one letter per square, both across and down, from the given clues. There will be a gray space between multi-word answers.

Tip: Solve the easy clues first, and then go back and answer the more difficult ones.

Across

2. the highest adult male singing voice; singing falsetto
4. the part of a song that transitions between two main parts
5. a combination of three or more tones sounded simultaneously
8. making up the song or melody as you play
11. a song written for one or more instruments playing solo
12. the highest of the singing voices
13. is a poem set to music with a recurring pattern of both rhyme and meter
14. timing or speed of the music

Down

1. singing without any instruments
3. low, the lowest of the voices and the lowest part of the harmony
6. to play a piece of music sweetly, tender, adoring manner
7. the sound of two or more notes heard simultaneously
9. is a musical interval; the distance between one note
10. played by a single musical instrument or voice
15. a range of voice that is between the bass and the alto
16. the repeating changing of the pitch of a note

CHORD   BRIDGE   ALTO
HARMONY   SOPRANO
IMPROVISATION   DOLCE
OCTAVE   VIBRATO   STANZA
SONATA   A CAPPELLA   TEMPO
BASS   SOLO   TENOR

4th Grade Health: The Food Groups

Eating healthy foods is especially important for children because they are still developing. Children's bodies require nutrition to develop strong, healthy _bones_ and muscles. You will not grow as tall or as strong as you could if you do not get all the _vitamins_ and minerals you require while growing.

Healthy food includes a wide variety of fresh foods from the five healthy food groups:

Dairy: Milk, cheese, and _yogurt_ are the most critical dairy foods, which are necessary for strong and healthy bones. There aren't many other foods in our diet that have as much calcium as these.

Fruit: Fruit contains vitamins, minerals, dietary fiber, and various phytonutrients (nutrients found naturally in plants) that help your body stay healthy. Fruits and vegetables provide you with energy, vitamins, antioxidants, fiber, and _water_. These nutrients help protect you against diseases later in life, such as heart disease, stroke, and some cancers.

Vegetables and legumes/beans: Vegetables should account for a large _portion_ of your daily food intake and should be encouraged at all meals (including snack times). To keep your body healthy, they supply vitamins, minerals, dietary fiber, and phytonutrients (nutrients found naturally in plants).

Grain (cereal) foods: choose wholegrain and/or high _fiber_ bread, cereals, rice, pasta, noodles, and so on. These foods provide you with the energy you require to grow, develop, and learn. Refined grain products (such as cakes and biscuits) can contain added sugar, fat, and sodium.

Protein from lean meats and poultry, fish, eggs, tofu, nuts and seeds, and legumes/beans is used by our bodies to _produce_ specialized chemicals such as hemoglobin and adrenalin. Protein also helps to build, maintain, and _repair_ tissues in our bodies. Protein is the primary component of muscles and organs (such as your heart).

Calories are a unit of measurement for the amount of energy in food. We gain calories when we eat, which gives us the energy to run around and do things. If we _consume_ more calories than we expend while moving, our bodies will store the excess calories as fat. If we burn more calories than we consume, our bodies will begin to burn the previously _stored_ fat.

4th Grade Environmental Health: Water Pollution

First, read the entire passage. After that, go back and fill in the blanks. You can skip the blanks you're unsure about and finish them later.

naturally	spills	toxic	crops	causes
streams	Gulf	wastewater	Acid	ill

Water pollution occurs when waste, chemicals, or other particles cause a body of water (e.g., rivers, oceans, lakes) to become __toxic__ to the fish and animals that rely on it for survival. Water pollution can also disrupt and hurt nature's water cycle.

Water pollution can occur __naturally__ due to volcanoes, algae blooms, animal waste, and silt from storms and floods.

Human activity contributes significantly to water pollution. Sewage, pesticides, fertilizers from farms, wastewater and chemicals from factories, silt from construction sites, and trash from people littering are some human __causes__ .

Oil __spills__ have been some of the most well-known examples of water pollution. The Exxon Valdez oil spill occurred when an oil tanker collided with a reef off the coast of Alaska, causing over 11 million gallons of oil to spill into the ocean. Another major oil spill was the Deepwater Horizon oil spill, which occurred when an oil well exploded, causing over 200 million gallons of oil to spill into the __Gulf__ of Mexico.

Water pollution can be caused directly by air pollution. When sulfur dioxide particles reach high altitudes in the atmosphere, they can combine with rain to form acid rain. __Acid__ rain can cause lakes to become acidic, killing fish and other animals.

The main issue caused by water pollution is the impact on aquatic life. Dead fish, birds, dolphins, and various other animals frequently wash up on beaches, killed by pollutants in their environment. Pollution also has an impact on the natural food chain. Small animals consume contaminants like lead and cadmium.

Clean water is one of the most valuable and essential commodities for life on Earth. Clean water is nearly impossible to obtain for over 1 billion people on the planet. They can become __ill__ from dirty, polluted water, which is especially difficult for young children. Some bacteria and pathogens in water can make people sick to the point of death.

Water pollution comes from a variety of sources. Here are a few of the main reasons:

Sewage: In many parts of the world, sewage is still flushed directly into __streams__ and rivers. Sewage can introduce dangerous bacteria that can make humans and animals very sick.

Farm animal waste: Runoff from large herds of farm animals such as pigs and cows can enter the water supply due to rain and large storms.

Pesticides: Pesticides and herbicides are frequently sprayed on __crops__ to kill bugs, while herbicides are sprayed to kill weeds. These potent chemicals can enter the water through rainstorm runoff. They can also contaminate rivers and lakes due to unintentional spills.

Construction, floods, and storms: Silt from construction, earthquakes, and storms can reduce water oxygen levels and suffocate fish. Factories - Water is frequently used in factories to process chemicals, keep engines cool, and wash things away. Sometimes used __wastewater__ is dumped into rivers or the ocean. It may contain pollutants.

4th Grade: Weather and Climate

The difference between weather and climate is simply a matter of time. Weather refers to the conditions of the atmosphere over a short period of time, whereas climate refers to how the atmosphere "behaves" over a longer period of time.

When we discuss climate change, we are referring to changes in long-term averages of daily weather. Today's children are constantly told by their parents and grandparents about how the snow was always piled up to their waists as they trudged off to school. Most children today have not experienced those kinds of dreadful snow-packed winters. The recent changes in winter snowfall indicate that the climate has changed since their parents were children.

Weather is essentially the atmosphere's behavior, particularly in terms of its effects on life and human activities. The distinction between weather and climate is that weather refers to short-term (minutes to months) changes in the atmosphere, whereas climate refers to long-term changes. Most people associate weather with temperature, humidity, precipitation, cloudiness, brightness, visibility, wind, and atmospheric pressure, as in high and low pressure.

Weather can change from minute to minute, hour to hour, day to day, and season to season in most places. However, the climate is the average of weather over time and space. A simple way to remember the distinction is that climate is what you expect, such as a very hot summer, whereas weather is what you get, such as a hot day with pop-up thunderstorms.

Use the word bank to unscramble the words!

Pressure	Density	Cloudy	Latitude	Elevation	Weather
Absorb	Humid	Precipitation	Windy	Forecast	Climate
Sunshine	Temperature				

IUMHD   Humid   8. LEICATM   Climate

UDLOYC   Cloudy   9. SNNIEHUS   Sunshine

FSEATOCR   Forecast   10. OBBASR   Absorb

UDLTITAE   Latitude   11. VETIEOANL   Elevation

IEOCAIIPPTRNT   Precipitation   12. EATWRHE   Weather

TEEERPAURMT   Temperature   13. NDWIY   Windy

RSEREUPS   Pressure   14. TYNEIDS   Density

4th Grade Life Skills: Peer Pressure

Almost all of us will come into contact with the apparent problem of peer pressure or the feeling that we have to do something because our friends or __classmates__ think it is cool. Peer pressure can be a serious issue, whether we're talking about first-graders being pressured to play games, they don't want to play, or college students being pressured to smoke or __drink__ alcohol. As you get older, you'll realize you're responsible for the peer pressure you're subjected to and inadvertently exert on others. Though you can never completely eliminate peer pressure, you can mitigate some of its negative effects.

Peers have an __impact__ on your life, even if you are unaware of it, simply by spending time with you. You learn from them, and they do the same for you. It's only natural to listen to and learn from people your own age.

Peers can have a __positive__ impact on one another. Perhaps another student in your science class taught you an easy way to remember the planets in the solar system, or someone on your soccer team taught you a cool ball trick. You might look up to a friend who is always a good sport and try to emulate him or her. Perhaps you piqued the interest of others in your new favorite book, and now everyone is reading it. These are examples of how peers positively __influence__ one another daily.

Peers can have a __negative__ influence on one another. For example, a few kids at school may try to persuade you to skip class with them, a soccer friend may try to convince you to be mean to another player and never pass the ball to her, or a kid in the neighborhood may try to persuade you to shoplift with him.

It is common for kids to fall __victim__ to the pressure of their peers because they want to be liked, to fit in, or because they are afraid that other kids will make fun of them if they don't follow suit. Others join in because they want to try something new that others are doing. The notion that "everyone is doing it" can lead some children to disregard their better judgment or common sense.

You've probably heard your parents or teachers tell you to "pick your friends wisely." Peer pressure is a major reason for this. If you choose friends who don't do drugs, skip class, smoke cigarettes, or lie to their parents, you're less likely to do the same, even if other kids do. Try to assist a friend who is __struggling__ to resist peer pressure. It can be powerful for one child to simply say, "I'm with you - let's go."

Even if you're alone and subjected to peer pressure, there are things you can do. You can __avoid__ peers who put you under pressure to do things you know are wrong. You can say "no" and walk away. Even better, find other friends and classmates to hang out with.

If you continue to experience peer pressure and find it challenging to deal with, talk to someone you __trust__. If you've made a mistake or two, don't feel bad about it. Talking to a parent, teacher, or school counselor can make you feel much better and prepare you for peer pressure the next time you are subjected to it.

ADDITIONAL ASSIGNMENTS PLANNER

○ MONDAY

GOALS THIS WEEK

○ TUESDAY

○ WEDNESDAY

WHAT TO STUDY

○ THURSDAY

○ FRIDAY

EXTRA CREDIT WEEKEND WORK
○ SATURDAY / SUNDAY

ADDITIONAL ASSIGNMENTS PLANNER

○ MONDAY

GOALS THIS WEEK

○ TUESDAY

○ WEDNESDAY

WHAT TO STUDY

○ THURSDAY

○ FRIDAY

EXTRA CREDIT WEEKEND WORK
○ SATURDAY / SUNDAY

ADDITIONAL ASSIGNMENTS PLANNER

○ MONDAY

○ TUESDAY

○ WEDNESDAY

○ THURSDAY

○ FRIDAY

EXTRA CREDIT WEEKEND WORK
○ SATURDAY / SUNDAY

GOALS THIS WEEK

WHAT TO STUDY

ADDITIONAL ASSIGNMENTS PLANNER

○ MONDAY

○ TUESDAY

○ WEDNESDAY

○ THURSDAY

○ FRIDAY

EXTRA CREDIT WEEKEND WORK
○ SATURDAY / SUNDAY

GOALS THIS WEEK

WHAT TO STUDY

GRADES TRACKER

Week	Monday	Tuesday	Wednesday	Thursday	Friday
1					
2					
3					
4					
5					
6					
7					
8					
9					
10					
11					
12					
13					
14					
15					
16					
17					
18					

Notes

GRADES TRACKER

Week	Monday	Tuesday	Wednesday	Thursday	Friday
1					
2					
3					
4					
5					
6					
7					
8					
9					
10					
11					
12					
13					
14					
15					
16					
17					
18					

Notes

End of the Year Evaluation

Name: _____

Grade/Level: _____ Date: _____

Subjects Studied: _____

_____

_____

Goals Accomplished: _____

_____

_____

_____

Most Improved Areas: _____

_____

_____

_____

Areas of Improvement: _____

_____

_____

Main Curriculum Evaluation	Satisfied	A= Above Standards S= Meets Standards N= Needs Improvement	Final Grades
_____	Yes No	98-100 A+ 93-97 A	_____
_____	Yes No	90-92 A 88-89 B+	_____
_____	Yes No	83-87 B 80-82 B	_____
_____	Yes No	78-79 C+ 73-77 C 70-72 C	_____
_____	Yes No	68-69 D+ 62-67 D	_____
_____	Yes No	60-62 D 59 & Below F	_____

Most Enjoyed: _____

_____

Least Enjoyed: _____

_____

Made in United States
Troutdale, OR
10/31/2024

24312612R00063